CW00925525

Freud and Fiction

Freud and Fiction

Sarah Kofman

Translated by Sarah Wykes

Polity Press

First published 1991 by Polity Press in association with Basil Blackwell

Editorial office:
Polity Press, 65 Bridge Street,
Cambridge CB2 1UR, UK

Marketing and production:
Basil Blackwell Ltd
108 Cowley Road, Oxford OX4 1JF, UK

ISBN 0 7456 0627 X

British Library Cataloguing in Publication Data
A CIP catalogue record for this book is available from the British Library.

Typeset in 11 on 13 pt Bembo
by Graphicraft Typesetters Ltd., Hong Kong
Printed in Great Britain by Billing and Sons Ltd., Worcester

Contents

Acknowledgements

The author and publishers wish to thank the following who have kindly given permission for the use of copyright material.

Basic Books, Inc. for extracts from *Sigmund Freud: Collected Papers, Volume 4*, translated under the supervision of Joan Riviere, by arrangement with The Hogarth Press, Ltd and the Institute of Psycho-Analysis, London; The Hogarth Press for extracts from *The Standard Edition of the Complete Psychological Works of Sigmund Freud*, edited and translated by James Strachey, 1953–66; Penguin Books Ltd for extracts from *Tales of Hoffmann*, translated by R. J. Hollingdale with Stella and Vernon Humphries, and Sally Hayward (Penguin Classics, 1982), copyright © Stella and Vernon Humphries, Sally Hayward and R. J. Hollingdale, 1982; Princeton University Press for extracts from *Complete Works of Aristotle: The Revised Oxford Translations*, edited by Jonathan Barnes, Bollingen Series 71, copyright © 1984 Jowett Copyright Trustees; Unwin Hyman Ltd for extracts from 'Delusion and Dreams in Jensen's Gravida' from *Complete Introductory Lectures on Psycho-Analysis* by Sigmund Freud.

Every effort has been made to trace all the copyright holders but if any have been inadvertently overlooked the publishers will be pleased to make the necessary arrangement at the first opportunity.

Translator's Preface

My particular thanks go to Marian Hobson Jeanneret and Chris Johnson for their encouragement and advice, to Jonathan Simon for his typing and to Lucy King. I would like to dedicate this translation to my family and my friends, without whose support it could not have been finished.

If in making these statements I have provoked the criticism, even from friends of psychoanalysis and those who are expert in it, that I have written a psychoanalytical novel [*bloss einen psychoanalytischen Roman geschrieben habe*], I shall reply that I am far from over-estimating the certainty of these results.

Freud, *Leonardo da Vinci and a Childhood Memory*

On the Analytic Novel

On the Analytic Novel

Freud the novelist

The four essays which follow,[1] grafted onto four of Freud's literary interpretations (of Empedocles' poems, Hebbel's *Judith*, Jensen's *Gradiva* and Hoffmann's *The Sandman*), are in fact rewritings of the texts from which they stem. In pushing the Freudian interpretation to its limits, in the most faithful way possible, they effect displacements which allow them, I feel, to 'surmount' a purely analytic kind of reading.

Initially, my reading of the works to which Freud refers was guided solely by a concern to further interpretation through the use of a comprehensive textual analysis; a necessary supplement given that in every case Freud, before he begins the task of interpretation, provides only a brief summary of the work in question. Reference to the text itself, in its entirety, brings the realization that the Freudian summary is not solely designed to refresh the reader's failing memory, but has a very specific methodological function: it is the condition of possibility of the interpretation at the same time as being its product. Freud may, in all modesty, claim not to change the work in any way but simply to 'gloss' a text which the author himself provides the commentary for. He may claim to be simply paraphrasing the text, elucidating it without making either additions or omissions. In fact, it seems that his readings of fictional works are in their turn fictions, 'romances' in their own right.

But would Freud have refused the title of novelist? The essential source of reference for his reconstruction of Leonardo da Vinci's childhood memory is a novel (Merzhkovshy's)[2] and Freud, 'far from over-estimating the certainty of his conclusions', predicts that 'friends of psychoanalysis' will accuse him of having written a 'psychoanalytical novel'.[3]

At the very least, Freud would recognize that he is a writer of novels, since he compares his analytic constructs to the delusions of his patients[4] and declares 'deep-rooted prejudices' to be the guiding and dominating force behind the most abstract speculations of philosophy and science. Science, offering only 'provisional validity', is, in his view, simply a mythology. Moreover, reasons of strategy could have made him claim the title of novelist: the notion of the 'analytic novel' could be an invaluable weapon against the dogmatism of those new believers whose adherence to psychoanalysis becomes a new catechism.

More generally, Freud always shows great modesty[5] when assessing the truth value of his method applied to fields other than pathology, notably to that of aesthetics. *The Moses of Michaelangelo*, for example, was written anonymously because Freud claimed it to be the result of a purely playful exercise carried out in an amateur capacity, expressing even stronger doubts than usual about his conclusions.[6]

However, it is not because Freudian readings of literary texts could be nothing more than mere hypotheses (and more than usually tenuous ones at that: deficient because lacking what is fundamental to the cure – the analysand's associations) that they are fictions. It is rather because, more than being detailed interpretations of a text they leave intact, they are in fact the constructs of a completely different text; rewritings which weave the thread of the elements in the original text into a completely new tissue, involving them by displacement in a completely different play. They are models, theoretical fictions which transform the initial untreated material of the text into a laboratory-controlled scientific fact which is capable of bending itself to analytic laws and categories.

The analytical novel is *methodical* (but then 'there is method in every madness'), a scientific or artistic method which progresses by means of dangerous short cuts, by a process of selection and torture of the text, by dissections, by dismemberments, in order, finally, to arrive at a hidden truth, concealed beneath the veil of a seductive beauty whose charms must be stripped away: the intervention of a whole process of translation, of formal and semantic changes, a violent 'mutilating, deforming and disfiguring' process which delivers up the original text in the form of a 'mutilated telegraph message', carrier of the analytic gospel. The last puts an end to the delusions and indecision of the text and brings the correct understanding of a sense that is finally univocal.

If on the one hand Freud recognizes the uncertainty of the scientific process and asserts the identity – or near identity – of science and fiction, on the other he accords high status to the author of fiction whom he takes to be a witness to the analytic truth. The writer's knowledge of this truth is obscure and endopsychic. In possessing it he or she resembles the superstitious, the deluded, certain primitive peoples. He or she is also, unwittingly, closer to psychoanalysis than rational science or psychiatry would be.

But here, in the guise of an admiring fascination, Freudian violence is once more in operation. The construction of theoretical fictions to make the literary text intelligible is the necessary complement to the role of crucial proof that this construction plays within an experimental method in which it, nevertheless, remains only a moment. The Freudian 'fiction' is a 'white lie', a bait to take the carp of truth.[7] This truth is that of the literary text which must confirm the truth of psychoanalysis. The violence consists in reducing the beauty of the text to a mere secondary 'effect' destined to disappear, to be '*relevé*'[8] in the process of the analytic truth. An effect of seduction, whose function is to ensnare and drug the reader, an effect the novel of analytic reason sets out to dispel, depriving the reader in the process of the free enjoyment [*jouissance*] of his or her fantasies: the function of the analytic fiction is *cathartic*.

If the transformation of the text were to be carried through to completion, its poetic and rhetorical 'effects' removed like veils, the metaphorical language of the text translated into the terms of metapsychology, what would remain of the literary text? Nothing. A negligible loss given that, in the course of unfolding the truth, all such 'effects' must disappear; a loss which is to be regretted only in terms of the ideological function society accords to works of art: a function of illusion. The illusion of art is, however, preferable to other forms of illusion (notably that of religion), and it is thanks to art that mankind can devote itself in all seriousness to the tasks of civilization. Art provides a privileged space, a playground at the heart of the world of culture where the adult can enjoy his or her fantasies without scruple, as she or he did as a child, experiencing a mixed pleasure, since in aesthetic pleasure the three psychic agencies, at all other times in conflict, are in harmony. It is precisely because art is a reconciliatory factor which disguises the 'discontents' of civilization, thereby helping to maintain it, that society makes the artist the equal of a god.

For Freud, the artist is a privileged being not because a bountiful nature has endowed him or her with creative 'gifts', but because he or she is able both to give and to experience pleasure to a greater extent than others. Privileged from an economic point of view, the artist is also, by the same token, granted the favour of humanity.

The function of the analytic novel is one of demystification: it ensures the death of the author as father of the text and denounces the contract of implicit pleasure between artist and public. However, if on the one hand Freud shatters the illusion of art, on the other he seems to consider this a necessary illusion for most people and one that is preferable to other forms of illusion. Only an elite is capable of the humour which allows one to bear the 'too heavy burden' of life without recourse to such illusions. Only an elite is capable of recognizing that the distinction between what is serious and what is play is a false one, that the serious is itself play.[9]

Moreover, one may question whether making a work of art intelligible is enough to prevent the discharge of affect it is supposed to produce, whether intelligibility, rather than eliminating pleasure, does not, in fact, increase it.

> Some of the grandest and most overwhelming creations of art are still unsolved riddles to our understanding. We admire them, we feel overawed by them, but we are unable to say what they represent to us. I am not sufficiently well-read to know whether this fact has been commented upon; possibly, indeed, some writer on aesthetics has discovered that this state of intellectual bewilderment is a necessary condition when a work of art is to achieve its greatest effects. It would only be with the greatest reluctance that I could bring myself to believe in any such necessity.[10]

In this case the pleasure which would be added to, or would replace, aesthetic pleasure would be the pleasure of knowledge. To a common pleasure in the fantastical, Freud adds the intellectual pleasure which stems from the resolution of the enigma which, for him, is the work of art; the pleasure which comes from grasping, detail by detail, the connections between a seemingly arbitrary 'creation' and the daily reality or past history of the artist.

But this pleasure can only be obtained via the mediation of the theoretical fiction which establishes a retrospective harmony between the work of art and the categories of analysis. Could the fantastical element which is at play in Freud's 'fictions' not be motivated, in fact, by the desire for this supplementary bonus? By the desire to see literary fiction corroborate analytic truth? And behind this desire, can we not recognize the workings of a fantasy of mastery and reappropriation of predecessors? A family romance in which ancestral prerogatives are recognized only in order to usurp them more successfully? A fantasy which keeps the author of fiction in a state of infancy, which condemns him to babble and stammer away until taken into guardianship by the father of psychoanalysis: 'A younger child is very specially inclined to use imaginative stories such as these in order to rob those born before them of their ancestral prerogatives – in a way which reminds one of historical intrigues.'[11]

Freud and philosophy

The family romance in which Freud turns literature into the infancy of psychoanalysis is not, however, his own personal fiction. It repeats the fiction invented by western metaphysics as a whole. Freud's gesture is related to the gesture of mastery which is symptomatic of philosophy, and a gesture Aristotle inaugurated by making myth the infancy of philosophy.

Freudian texts are evidently complex and must be read carefully, as I showed in *L'Enfance de l'Art.*[12] By distinguishing what Freud *does* from what he *says*, we can see that his texts do indeed lead to the deconstruction of metaphysics. However, these same texts concur with the texts of the whole of philosophical tradition and can, genealogically speaking, be classified as *philosophical.* This is particularly notable in the case of Freud's readings of literary texts. Taking as their point of departure the effect or affect produced and tracing it back, according to the analytic method, to an underlying cause, the repressed ideational content (to be revealed or constructed), they are *thematic* readings, dependent on a form–content opposition, based on metaphysical categories of true and false and on what is called 'the traditional logic of the sign'. Freudian interpretations involve the same notion of the 'effect' as philosophy: the 'effect' is precisely what philosophy claims to reduce or to dispense with.

In order to emphasize this crossover between psychoanalysis and philosophy I feel it would be relevant to preface my essays with a brief recap of Aristotle's reading of the presocratic philosophers. This reading is paradigmatic of all philosophical interpretation and was subsequently endorsed and repeated by other philosophers, including Hegel, right up to Nietzsche. Nietzsche was the first to form a different conception of the earliest philosophers to the accepted Aristotelian one and to show that they are of a rare type, one which cannot be reduced to any other. By 'painting them a hundred times on the wall',[13] he reconstructed an image which had been disfigured by the whole of philosophical tradition.

Aristotle and the 'presocratics'

> Aristotle is our most abundant authority; he studied the older philosophers expressly and most thoroughly and he has, in the beginning of his *Metaphysics* especially, and also to a large extent elsewhere, dealt with them in historical order: he is as philosophic as erudite and we may rely upon him. We can do no better in Greek philosophy than study the first book of his *Metaphysics*.
>
> Hegel, *Introduction to the Lectures on the History of Philosophy*[14]

> Between the great man of the concept, Aristotle, and the customs (*Sitte*) and art of the Hellenes, there is the greatest gulf.
>
> Nietzsche, *Einleitung in das Studium der Classischen Philologie*[15]

In Book A of his *Metaphysics* Aristotle makes a reading of his predecessors (not only the 'presocratic' philosophers, but also Plato, so that they should in fact be referred to as 'prearistotelian') which has been the inheritance of the whole of western philosophy. Since he sets out to determine 'what is good in their views and what is bad';[16] which of their ideas can be 'retained' in terms of Aristotelian truth, his reading can be termed 'reductive'.

The reduction consists in 'taking' (λαμβὰνειν (lambanein), cf. 985ab, 986b, 987a) from the presocratic thinkers what he recognizes elsewhere to be ungraspable and irreducible: their qualities of ingenuity and brilliance, their originality as inscribed in the metaphorical style of their texts. Indeed, 'the greatest thing by far is to be a master of metaphor. It is one thing that cannot be learnt from others and it is also a sign of genius.'[17]

Just as Aristotle subordinates metaphor to concept, so he subordinates his predecessors to his authority: an exercise of mastery analogous to that mastery which, in the *Politics*, he declares it natural for master to exercise over slave, father over child, male over female, Greek over barbarian. In this case, however, we are dealing with more than an analogy. On the one hand the concept as literal, 'proper' sense as opposed to figurative sense is **κυρίον** (kurion), 'the propriety of a name utilized in its dominant, master, capital sense':[18] the master word that dominates other derivative or merely metaphorical senses. On the other hand, only the master, the father, the man, the Greek has the right to the word, to speech,[19] to the logos. The ontological hierarchy functions according to the greater or lesser degree to which the substantial form of the essence is perfected. It stretches from plant life at one end of the scale to God at the other, passing through animals and human beings, and, within the structure of the human world, from the slave to the philosopher via the barbarian, the woman and the child. Running parallel to it is another hierarchy based on the possession or non-possesion of the rational principle and the power of speech. At the summit is the philosopher, in whom reason reaches its highest degree of perfection, and at the bottom plants and animals, which cannot speak. Between these two extremes lie the slave, whose speech merely echoes his master's, the barbarian who 'croaks', the child who stammers[20] and the woman whose greatest virtue is her reserve in speech, her silence.[21]

If, within this hierarchy, there are some beings whose inferiority is indelible and essential, such as the woman, there are also, conversely, beings whose inferiority is merely provisional. The male child is a potential man, his stammering is the seed of man's language: the male child is a little man. In the same way, metaphorical or mythical language, the language of infancy, is philosophical language in potentiality: metaphors already prefigure, albeit imperfectly, concepts.

Just as the male child is matter from which the future man emerges, a potentiality of indeterminate contraries that only form can actualize and make determinate, so the metaphorical language of philosophy's dawn is indeterminate matter: a language to which only the philosophical conceptual language that gives it form can give a clear, precise sense.

Whilst it is the case that chronologically (in one sense at least)[22] potentiality and matter are prior to actuality and form, ontologically, the latter take precedence. They command and control, they alone can give definite and determinate sense to what precedes them.

Thus, in its infancy, philosophical thought had to begin by stammering in a metaphorical language. This means both that metaphorical language is inferior to conceptual language (only the latter brings to actuality the truth which metaphor contains in potentiality) and that it is in itself already a form of truth, a potential, indeterminate, obscure truth, concealing a logos that is hidden, not articulated. Originary, metaphorical writing, far from being, as it is for Nietzsche, the symptom of an affirmative, flourishing and full life, is a sign of immaturity, of an auroral state of imperfection that nevertheless already contains within it the seed of Aristotelian truth.

Metaphor is proper to man (his property and propriety)[23] because it is already a meaning which mimics by analogy the true meaning: 'for metaphor does make what it signifies to some extent familiar because of the likeness involved' (*Topics*, VI, 2, 139b–140a). Likewise myth involves a search for knowledge and 'even the lover of myths is in a sense a lover of wisdom' (καὶ ὁ φιλόμῦθος φιλόσοφός πώς ἐστιν) (*Metaphysics*, A, 982). The operation in mastery consists in the assertion that preceding philosophers are only interesting in so far as they herald and confirm the Aristotelian truth. All the rest is empty literature. The violence consists in imposing the *archè* (αρχη) of philosophy and of the logos on myth and metaphor, in absorbing the individual genius of each philosopher into the identity of Aristotelian doctrine.

This would account for Aristotle's double evaluation of preceding thinkers: they constituted a stage which had to be passed, and their theories should be given careful consideration, just as commonplace opinions which are more or less coherent should be studied since they conceal a certain truth. On the other hand, without the perfected science which transforms an indeterminate and polysemous language into a transparent and univocal language, their theories remain incomplete. Polysemia, with its excess of sense, is equivalent to an absence of sense. Saying something that has several senses comes to mean saying nothing properly, to being like a plant: 'We can, however, demonstrate negatively that even this view [that something is and is not] is impossible, if our opponent will only say something; and if he says nothing, it is absurd to attempt to reason with one who will not reason about anything, in so far as he refuses to reason. For such a man, as such, is seen already to be not better than a mere plant' (*Topics*, T4, 1006a, 12–15).

True, philosophical language, should have only one sense, its proper sense. Thus Plato, in using the poetic metaphor of the term 'participation', spoke to say nothing. Of itself this word has no sense; it is empty matter, female waiting for the male to come and fill her, to master her by subjugating her to the proper sense, to his sense, to the master- or master's-sense: 'to say that they [the ideas] are patterns and the other things share in them is to use empty words and poetical metaphors' (*Metaphysics*, A9, 991a).

Between actual and potential knowledge there is both continuity and rupture. Continuity, because the former is the finality, the perfection of the latter, the completion of its incompletion. Rupture, because there is no common measure between the lowest and the highest degrees of the hierarchy; instead there is a truly qualitative leap.

The true or proper sense imposes its law (the *nous* is the *nomos*), is self-enlightened, it reveals itself to itself[24] without needing the inferior degrees on which, nevertheless, to some degree, it has depended. Thus philosophy is both a part of the system of knowledge and at the same time all that there is to know, the only knowledge worthy of that name: it imposes its name on all the other parts of the system. The dominant does not stand in a relation of genus to species to that which it dominates. There is no generic unity between philosophy and what is subordinate to it, just as there is no generic unity between the different parts of the soul nor anywhere where there is a hierarchy and something resembling an anterior–posterior relation.

Despite this, only the divinity, thought which reflects upon itself,[25] possesses knowledge in actuality. Only the divinity is the perfect philosopher and absolute master. Because Aristotle, like every other philosopher, no matter how close to the divine he might be, is not God, his own knowledge can never be more than a potentiality, and he needs his predecessors to testify to the truth of his doctrine; predecessors from whom he can always 'take'[26] something since, being men, they all already, to some degree, speak the truth. It is man's specific state to be neither a fool nor a wise man, but to be potentially wise. This intermediate condition explains the existence of a history of philosophy and the fact that this history is understood according to a biological model as the development of an initial seed: 'no one is able to obtain the truth adequately, while, on the other hand, no one fails entirely, but everyone says something about the nature of things, and . . . by the union of all a considerable amount is amassed' (*Metaphysics*, 11a, 993a–b).

Thus to make the history of philosophy is to bring to light the truth which lies hidden in, and obscured by, the doctrines of previous philosophers, to articulate it by bringing it from a state of infancy to maturity. Far from accusing Aristotle of the theft of what is unique and original to them, the earliest thinkers would, if they were able, thank him for having raised their writings to such a high level.

Paradoxically, it is through the use of a system of three metaphors that Aristotle 'brings to light' the relation he establishes between his own theories and those of his predecessors.

Firstly the metaphor of light: 'for a metaphorical expression is always obscure (ἀσαφες)' (*Topics*, VI, 139b). The writings of the earliest thinkers are obscure because they 'touch' the truth more than 'see' it, because the multiple senses of metaphorical terms are fused in an intimate contact, copulating with one another. As yet the gaze of philosophy has not intervened to impose its law on chaos and to establish a discriminating distance. There is the same difference between Aristotelian and presocratic philosophy as between a noble sense, whose ideal is to be pure 'theory', and a servile sense that is accustomed to work by means of contact with matter. Or, again, the vision of the presocratics is compared to the vision of a bat, while philosophy is said to have the piercing eye of the lynx, a penetrating gaze, a perfected vision: to know is not to operate on matter using tools, but to discriminate. A noble task, yet one which depends on the work of the slave. Thus to pass from a metaphorical to conceptual philosophy is to pass from obscurity into light, to move from the indeterminate to the distinct. But the lack of distinctions means a return to the originary chaos in which everything is mixed together: a return to the infancy of philosophy when philosophers both did and did not speak the truth (for example, that the good is the cause, cf. 988b).

The metaphor of infancy is always used in tandem with that of obscurity. To pass from obscurity into light is to acquire the eye of judgement, the adult eye introducing the law of discrimination that simultaneously regulates infantile desires and the confusion of senses: 'we have learnt this much from them [the earliest thinkers], that of those who speak about principle and cause no one has mentioned any principle except those which have been distinguished in our work on nature, but all evidently have some inkling (θιγγάνοντες touched, felt) of them, though only vaguely (ἀμυδρῶς in a non-articulated way)'[27] (*Metaphysics*, A, 988a).

> It is evident, then, that even from what we have said before, that all men seem to seek the causes named in the *Physics* and that we cannot name any beyond these; but they seek these vaguely; and though in a sense they have all been described before in another sense they have not been described at all. For the earliest philosophy is, on all subjects, like one who lisps, since in its beginnings it is but a child. (*Metaphysics*, A, 10, 993a)

But the adult eye, no matter how perfect its vision, is still not the eye of God. Clarity can only be obtained by adding together the insights and ideas[28] each man has to contribute, just as the painter can only paint a beautiful portrait by combining aspects from several different models, and political truth is the result of consultation of the multitude. In isolation, no man is beautiful or knows the truth. The ideal of the philosopher would be to an Argus with a hundred eyes.

> The investigation of truth is in one way hard, in another easy. An indication of this is found in the fact that no one is able to attain the truth adequately, while, on the other hand, no one fails entirely, but everyone says something true about the nature of things, and whilst individually they contribute little or nothing to the truth, by the union of all a considerable amount is amassed. Therefore, since the truth seems to be like the proverbial door which no one can fail to hit, in this sense it is easy, but the fact that we can have a whole truth and not the particular part we aim at shows the difficulty of it.
>
> Perhaps, as difficulties are of two kinds, the cause of the present difficulty is not in the facts but in us. For as the eyes of bats are to the blaze of day, so is the reason in our soul to the things which are by nature most evident of all. It is just that we should be grateful, not only to those whose opinions we may share, but also to those who have expressed more

superficial views; for these also contributed something by developing before us the powers of thought. It is true that if there had been no Timotheus we should have been without much of our lyric poetry; but if there had been no Phrynis, there would have been no Timotheus. The same holds good of those who have expressed views about the truth: for from the better thinkers we have inherited certain opinions, while the others have been responsible for the appearance of the better thinkers. (*Metaphysics*, 993b)

For the many, of whom each individual is not a good man, when they meet together may be better than the few good, if regarded not individually but collectively, just as a feast to which many contribute is better than a dinner provided out of a single purse. For each individual among the many has a share of excellence and practical wisdom, and when they meet together, just as they become in a manner one man who has many feet and hands, so too with regard to their character and thought. Hence the many are better judges than a single man of music and poetry; for some understand one part and some another, and between them they understand the whole.

There is a similar combination of qualities in good men, who differ from any individual of the many, as the beautiful are said to differ from those who are not beautiful, and works of art from realities, because in them the scattered elements are combined, although if taken separately the eye of one person would be fairer than that in the picture. (*Politics*, III, 1281b).

Aristotle adds to the metaphors of obscurity and infancy that of the untrained soldier:

These thinkers, as we say, evidently got hold, up to a certain point, of two of the causes which we distinguished in our work on nature – the nature of matter and the source of movement – but only vaguely and with no clarity (ἀμυδρῶς καὶ οὐθεν σαφῶς) as untrained men behave in fights; for they go round their opponents and often strike fine blows, but they do not fight on scientific principles and likewise these thinkers do not seem to know what they say; for it is evident that, as a rule, they make no use of their causes except to a small extent. (*Metaphysics*, A, 985a)

If philosophy in its infancy is in a state of obscurity, it is because thought has not been sufficiently trained. The ability to think is both a natural gift and the result of an apprenticeship. History is the training ground of the intellect where the ability to think is developed and realizes itself, passing from potentiality to actuality. The same applies to thought as to virtue; it is both natural and something which develops with practice: 'one swallow does not make a summer',[29] practice makes perfect;[30] thinking makes a thinker. The training that is necessary if thought is to master itself is that unavoidable share of slavery which stems from the fact that a man is a man and not a god.

Because the earliest thinkers 'do not know what they are saying', being unaware of the truth they possess, their texts must be interpreted, the hidden truth extracted from or inserted into them, by reducing the equivocality of meaning to a single univocal sense, by eliminating everything that cannot be traced back to this truth as excessive, a negligible, an infantile remainder.

Thus it is hardly surprising, after such forcing, to find in the texts of one's predecessors confirmation of the truth of one's own doctrine. By taking refuge behind the obscurity and immaturity of the earliest thinkers, Aristotle is free to distinguish what they actually said from 'what they meant to say' and to slip his own theories into the gap between the two, claiming nevertheless to find them always already present, waiting to be discovered:

We have discussed these matters more exactly elsewhere. But the object of our discussion is that we may learn from these philosophers also what they suppose to be the principles and how these fall under the causes we have named. (*Metaphysics*, 986a)

All these thinkers, then, as they cannot pitch on anther cause, seem to testify that we have determined rightly both how many and of what sort the causes are. (Ibid., 988b)

As regards Anaxagoras, if one were to suppose that he said there were two elements, the supposition would accord thoroughly with a view which Anaxagoras himself did not state articulately, but which he must have accepted if anyone had developed his view . . . yet if one were to follow him up, piecing together what he means, he would perhaps be seen to be somewhat modern in his views. (Ibid., 989b)

But while he [Empedocles] would necessarily have agreed if another had said this, he has not said it clearly (σαφῶς). (Ibid., 993a)

An abuse of force on texts whose fathers are no longer there to defend them; in such a manner Aristotle recognizes that writing is an orphan, but does so only to subject it immediately to his tutelage by reinscribing his predecessors' texts into the process of the Aristotelian truth: the truth which is the *archè*, the final cause of the whole development: the father, keeper of the truth, is at the end but directs and commands every part of the process:

when these men and the principles of this kind had had their day, as the latter were found inadequate to generate the nature of things, men were again forced by truth itself, as we said, to inquire into the next kind of cause. (*Metaphysics*, 984a)

among existing things there must be a cause which will move things and bring them together. (Ibid., 984b)

for claiming that, besides the existent nothing non-existent exists, he [Parmenides] thinks that the existent is of necessity one and that nothing else exists (on this we have spoken more clearly in our work on nature) but being forced to follow the phenomena and supposing that what is is one in formula but many in perception, he now posits two causes and two principles. (Ibid., 986b)

In this fashion Aristotle inaugurates a conception of the history of philosophy, of history to which the whole of metaphysics has been in thrall. According to this notion history is always the history of the truth, of its development, of the 'relève'[31] of one philosopher by another, of one untrained soldier by another, better trained one. But, because no philosopher is God, the break between the logos and the myth is never completely achieved; the philosopher continues to be always somewhat of a 'liar', a poet (cf. *Metaphysics*, 983a). Aristotle himself can only illustrate the opposition between myth and philosophy, metaphor and concept, by the use of a series of metaphor, and 'this entire philosophical delimitation of metaphor already lends itself to being constructed and worked by metaphors.'[32] Theory is itself simply a metaphor and the language of philosophy remains a language of analogy. Only the divinity, if it were to speak, would speak properly. But, of course, it does not speak (the logos is proper to man, the political animal) but contemplates itself narcissistically, thought reflecting upon itself into infinity.

Aristotle's metaphors constitute a secondary text within the text which undermines its authority and its seriousness by introducing an element of play into it. Subsequent philosophical tradition seems hardly to have been aware of this play, seems even to have occulted it. With the utmost seriousness, it reiterates Aristotle's reading of the presocratics and, more generally, claims its authority from his (an anti-cathexis to philosophy's repressed?), going even further than he did in its gesture of mastery.

Freud and Empedocles

Empedocles is more poetic than definitely philosophical; he is not very interesting, and much cannot be made of his philosophy.

Hegel, *Lectures on the History of Philosophy*

It is a real misfortune that so very little of these older philosophic masters has come down to us and that all complete works of theirs are withheld from us . . . some people presuppose a special providence for books . . . such a providence however would at any rate be a very malicious one if it deemed it wise to withhold from us the works of Heraclitus, Empedocles's marvellous poems . . .

Nietzsche, *Philosophy During the Tragic Age of the Greeks*

This made me all the more pleased when not long ago I came upon this theory of mine in the writings of one of the great thinkers of ancient Greece . . . Empedocles of Acragus (Grigenti), born about 495 BC, is one of the grandest and most remarkable figures in the history of Greek civilisation.

Freud, *Analysis Terminable and Interminable*

Freud and Empedocles

A seductive analogy

It may seem paradoxical to compare Freud to Empedocles, the fifth-century BC Greek philosopher. However, such a comparison is not arbitrary since it is Freud himself who instigates it. He is seduced[1] by the personality of the philosopher he describes in *Analysis Terminable and Interminable* as 'one of the grandest and most remarkable figures in the history of Greek civilisation' and captivated by Empedocles' doctrine, as he states on several occasions in his final works, especially in the *New Introductory Lectures*, in *An Outline of Psychoanalysis* and above all in *Analysis Terminable and Interminable.*

In the *New Introductory Lectures*, whilst expounding his new theory of the instincts, he suggests an analogy with Schopenhauer's theory. Schopenhauer's Will to Life reminds him of Eros, the life instinct, and Schopenhauer's 'self-denial of the Will' reminds him of the death instincts. Then Freud adds: 'moreover, there is nothing that has not been said already, and similar things had been said by many people before Schopenhauer' (*New Introductory Lectures*, p. 107). If the reference to Empedocles is not made explicit, the following note in a text of Schopenhauer's removes any doubt: 'for, as Empedocles says, if strife did not rule in things, then all would be unity' (*The World as Will and Representation*).[2]

In the second chapter of *An Outline of Psychoanalysis*, again outlining his theory of the instincts, their aims and biological functioning, and proposing the extension of his theory into the physical sphere, Freud adds the following note: 'This picture of the basic forces or instincts, which still arouses much opposition amongst analysts, was already familiar to the philosopher Empedocles of Acragas' (*An Outline of Psychoanalysis*, p. 149).

In *Analysis Terminable and Interminable*, Freud deplores the difficulties he has encountered in trying to get his new idea of the death instinct accepted, even among analysts, and he describes his pleasure at finding that this notion had already been explored in the writings of Empedocles. The resemblance between the two theories seems so remarkable to him that he even suggests an instance of cryptoamnesia, adding that 'we should be tempted to maintain that the two [theories] are identical' (p. 245). A few paragraphs later he writes: 'The two fundamental principles of Empedocles – 'φιλία' and 'νεῖκος' – are, both in name and function the same as our two primal instincts (*Urtriebe*), Eros and destructiveness, the first of which endeavours to combine what exists into ever greater unities, while the second endeavours to dissolve these combinations and to destroy the structures (*Gebilde*) to which they have given rise' (pp. 245–6).

Nevertheless, he considers it to be quite normal that 'on its reemergence after two and a half millennia' (p. 246), Empedocles' theory should have undergone some changes. The most important of these changes relates to the status of the theory's truth: mythical in the Empedoclean version (Freud refers to it as a 'cosmic fantasy'), it is meant in the Freudian version to be scientific. Moreover, the scope of the Empedoclean theory is reduced from the cosmic to the biophysical. Freud can no longer accept all Empedocles' claims. The four elements (earth, water, fire, air) can no longer be posited as the primary universal substances; living matter is not identical to inanimate matter; the combination and separation of particles of matter is replaced by the fusion and disintegration of instinctual components. Finally,

Freud claims to give a biological basis to the duality of the Empedoclean cosmic principles and particularly to the principle of strife 'by tracing back our instinct of destruction to the death instinct, to the urge of what is living to return to an inanimate state' (ibid.).

Some of these differences can, however, be reduced. The Empedoclean cosmos, though eternal, is a living entity conceived on the model of an individual living organism, and the two governing principles of the universe, love and hate,[3] locked in eternal conflict, are neither intelligent forces with a conscious purpose nor purely mechanical. In fact, they can be compared to biophysical instincts. According to Freud they are 'natural forces operating like instincts'.

Moreover, in formulating his theory of the existence of a universal death instinct, one which would be in existence prior even to life itself and which would be revealed by physical phenomena such as the repulsion of bodies, Freud gives his own theory a cosmic dimension. The reduction of Empedocles' cosmic theory to a biological level and the theoretical extension of Freud's theory from a biophysical to a cosmic level bring the two even closer together, and lead Freud to conclude that 'no one can foresee in what way the nucleus of truth contained in the theory of Empedocles will present itself to later understanding'.

The privilege of myth

But why does Freud place so much emphasis on this link with Empedocles? Is it simply the case that, having encountered resistance to his new theory of the instincts in his immediate circle, he draws comfort from finding it expressed elsewhere? Or does his insistence stem from a concern for intellectual integrity? In effect, he states on several occasions his indifference to questions of priority and originality and mentions that his theory can be found already formulated in the work of philosophers such as Plato, Schopenhauer and Nietzsche. But he does so only to claim that this is why he has avoided reading these philosophers – to avoid any form of bias and to ensure that his speculations are based on the results of empirical observation alone. 'It is of no concern to us in this connection to inquire how far, with this hypothesis of the pleasure principle, we have approached or adopted any particular, historically established philosophical system. We have arrived at these speculative assumptions in an attempt to describe and to account for the facts of daily observation in our field of study.'[4]

> Even when I have moved away from observation I have carefully avoided any contact with philosophy proper. This avoidance has been greatly facilitated by constitutional incapacity ... The large extent to which psychoanalysis coincides with the philosophy of Schopenhauer ... is not to be traced to my acquaintance with his teaching. I read Schopenhauer very late in my life. Nietzsche, another philosopher whose guesses and intuitions often agree in the most astonishing way with the various findings of psychoanalysis, was for a long time avoided by me on that very account; I was less concerned with the question of primacy than with keeping my mind unembarrassed.[5]

Thus the importance Freud attaches to Empedocles seems exceptional, privileged and, by the same token, problematic. In my view the fundamental reason behind Freud's interest is that he sees the possibility of making the Empedoclean myth play an exemplary role: it would be to his third theory of the instincts what the Oedipus myth was to his second topic. Indeed, according to Freudian interpretation, the Empedoclean myth results from the unconscious projection of the instincts, both unconsious and distorted by displacement from a biological to a cosmic level. Freud's theory of the instincts would reduce the cosmic and mythical content to its psychic reality.[6] Freud would merely be applying to the specific case of Empedocles his general interpretation of myth and speculative metaphysical or religious constructions. Like superstitious or certain paranoiac constructions, the latter are the projection of unconscious instinctual drives into external forces. Thus Freud defines metapsychology as an attempt to correct metaphysical constructions:

> I believe that a large part of the mythological view of the world, which extends a long way into the most modern religions, *is nothing but psychology projected into the external world*. The obscure recognition (the endopsychic projection, as it were) of psychical factors and relations in the unconscious is mirrored ... in the construction of a *supernatural reality*, which is destined to be changed back once more by science into the *psychology of the unconscious* ... One could venture ... to transform *metaphysics* into *metapsychology*.[7]

As the unconscious projection of the instincts, distorted by displacement, into the external world, the Empedoclean myth would simultaneously reveal and conceal psychic truth. Freud, by giving the myth a biopsychic basis, effectively operates an inversion from the exterior to the interior and, by the same token, passes from myth to science. Empedocles' cosmological myth testifies to the natural character of culture and in it culture finds its conditions of possibility in such a way that Freud can read it in the back-projected light of what it itself has allowed.

Henceforth it is easy to understand why Freud favours Empedocles. What is determining here is the mythical element. In as far as every myth contains a psychic truth, a mythical philosophy is more symptomatic, more revealing of the unconscious and closer to primary processes than a purely speculative philosophy would be, since the latter is the product of more sophisticated secondary rationalizations, speaking the language of the secondary processes, and claiming to voice the truth clearly and distinctly. By concealing, myth reveals more than the supposed conceptual clarity of the philosophers. And if Freud selects Empedocles from all the mythicizing philosophers, preferring him to, for example, Plato, to whom he makes several references (and always to the mythical aspects of his writing, in particular to the myth of Aristophanes in the *Symposium*), it is primarily because Empedocles is the only one to ascribe a double causality to all things. But it is also because Empedocles' writings have survived only in a fragmentary form. In fact, of the 5000 verses he wrote, only 400 verses of the *Physics* and 120 verses of his *Katharmoi* have been preserved.[8]

This fragmentary character is itself, in effect, already an image of the lacunal character of the psychic self. Finally, the very duality of the work, which is composed of two poems, one seemingly scientific, the other quasi-mystical, expressing perfectly the duality of the instincts and the essentially ambiguous personality of Empedocles, could not fail to fascinate Freud. In *Analysis Terminable and Interminable*, Freud justly emphasizes Empedocles' 'many-sided personality': Empedocles was at once an investigator and a thinker, a prophet and a magician, a politician, a philanthropist and a doctor versed in the natural sciences. Exact and precise in his research into physics and physiology, yet at the same time mystical, obscure, fond of popular superstitions and religion, believing in an animate universe and the transmigration of souls.[9]

Speculation

But there is another reason why Freud refers to a mythical philosophy, to Empedoclean doctrine in particular, and why he does so each time he explains his theory of the instincts. For whilst it is indeed the case that psychic reality is the true content of the myth, it could also be said that the Empedoclean myth serves as a substitute, a possibly provisional substitute, for a completely rational basis to Freud's final theory of the instincts. This can be imagined as a circle: the theory of instincts establishes the truth of the Empedoclean myth, which in turn acts as proof of the validity of the former. There is a reciprocal relationship between myth and theory in which each is the verification of the other: a circularity in which each retains its hypothetical character. Freud makes it clear that myth is used as a substitute for science in *Beyond the Pleasure Principle*: 'What we cannot reach flying we must reach limping' (SE, p. 64).

Freud's recourse to myth signifies that the radical conflict at the root of psychic life can never be directly perceived, that it only reveals itself obliquely, through, for example, the conflicts between the psychic agencies. The underlying cause of all conflicts and of their continued existence, which is forever irreducible, this antagonism is itself without rational explanation, pure, brute fact which cannot be explained by any rational concept. The recourse to myth reveals the mystery of this antagonism, which can be posited only as an anhypothesis beyond which it is impossible to go, a foundation without foundation, unless it be mythical.

In effect, speculation of a scientific or economic nature is of little help in this case. In *Analysis Terminable and Interminable* Freud shows that masochism, the negative therapeutic reaction, and the sense of guilt found in neurotics, prove that the pleasure principle alone cannot sufficiently account for all the phenomena of mental life. These phenomena lead him to postulate the existence of a force which he calls, in view of its aims, the instinct of aggression or destruction. This instinct derives its source from the death instinct inherent in living matter: 'Only by the concurrent or mutually opposing action of the two primal instincts – Eros and the death instinct – never by one or the other alone, can we explain the rich multiplicity of the phenomena of life' (*Analysis Terminable and Interminable*, p. 243). Freud then asks himself how elements of these two kinds of instinct combine to carry out the various vital functions, how such combinations are formed or dissolved and what kinds of disturbance ensue from these changes. Taking bisexuality as an example, he shows that an economic explanation could be envisaged: there may be only a certain amount of libido available and the two opposing tendencies must struggle for it. In effect, in certain instances it seems as if the libido is divided without conflict. The question then arises of why this is not so in every case. Freud concludes that 'the tendency to a conflict is something special . . . irrespective of the quantity of libido' (ibid., p. 244).

Henceforth, the notion of psychic conflict must be completely rethought. It is only comprehensible if inscribed into the life instinct is its opposite, its other, its negativity: what Freud calls the death instinct, of equal force to Eros, a principle of internal inhibition. Previously, Freud's dualism was located at the level of the aims and objects of the instincts, not within the instincts themselves. With the theory of the death instinct, this dualism becomes radical: 'Our views have from the very first been *dualistic* and today they are even more definitely (*schärfer*) dualistic than before – now that we describe the opposition as being not between ego instincts and sexual instincts, but between life instincts and death instincts' (*Beyond the Pleasure Principle*, SE, XVIII, p. 53).

Between Freud's initial dualism and his final version it is not simply a question of a difference in degree, but of a difference in kind: with the theory of the death instinct, Freud reveals the very root, the foundation, of all duality, all conflict and of their irreducible nature.

But this anhypothetical hypothetical explanation is itself mythical, in the sense that the death instinct can never be perceived directly, but only indirectly, through observation and clinical facts: for which in the final analysis other explanations can always be found. In effect, the death instinct is a subterranean force; it operates in silence and most of the time it cannot be distinguished from its opponent, Eros (inexhaustible source of tensions, operating in 'the clamour of life')[10], so much so that for a long time it successfully eluded Freudian vigilance: 'The instinctual forces which seek to conduct life into death may also be operating in protozoa from the first, and yet their effects may be so completely concealed by the life preserving forces that it may be very hard to find any direct evidence of their presence.'[11]

The death instinct is mute, or speaks obliquely via signs: expressions which are only its partial and inadequate representatives. In the *New Introductory Lectures* Freud describes the 'mute and uncanny activity of the death instincts' (p. 109); in *An Outline of Psychoanalysis* he adds: 'So long as that instinct operates internally, as a death instinct, it remains silent; it only comes to our notice when it is diverted outwards as an instinct of destruction' (p. 150).

For this reason Freud speaks of death instincts, in the plural, rather than of a death instinct: the latter cannot, so to speak, even be named. Its most obvious derivations and representatives are the tendency to inertia and to repetition, in this sense the general form of all instincts, the instinct of aggression, negation. Negation, which according to Freud in *Die Verneinung*[12] 'belongs to the instinct of destruction', seems, on the level of the secondary processes of the conscious, to be the least reducible to any other explanation and the most revealing about the nature of the death instinct as a principle of negativity internal to the instinct, one which, by this very fact, can only be read as the finitude of a certain positivity or in the infinitude of desire which is its anticathexis. Thus we begin to understand why Freud avails himself of the Empedoclean myth at the moment when he expounds his new theory of the instincts and in particular when he is outlining his notion of the death instinct. To this a final reason must be added: the Empedoclean myth provides a model for the extension of his hypothesis into all domains of the biological[13] and the physical[14] world, giving it a cosmic dimension that is not justified by any real scientific evidence. The changes in the Freudian terminology are characteristic in this respect: Eros is a term which has much greater significance than libido, ἀνάγκη is the principle of necessity he borrows directly from Empedocles. However, if he does not speak of θάνατος but of death instincts – which may seem paradoxical, given that the death instinct is much more a principle of psychic functioning than a class of instinct that can be observed and distinguished in terms of a source, an object and an aim – it is because here the principle itself cannot be reduced to any nomination: any nomination could only misrepresent it.

The speculative character of the final theory of the instincts, which requires the recourse to myth to fill the lacunae left by science, is clearly indicated in all the Freudian texts. In *Beyond the Pleasure Principle* Freud states: 'What follows is speculation, often far-fetched speculation.'[15] Further on he says that if his hypothesis, that all instincts tend to reproduce a previously existing state of things, were taken to its ultimate conclusion, then it would mean his risking being branded a mystic. For this reason he declares that he is seeking only the actual results of empirical research and will base his speculation on these results alone. Nevertheless, the obscurity which reigns over the theory of the instincts does not allow him to reject the slightest glimmer of an explanation, even if it is mythical. Thus science in no way allows him to affirm the repetitive and regressive nature of the life instincts: it is only in the myths he calls 'fantastical' that such hypotheses can be found, whether in the myth of Aristophanes in Plato's *Symposium*, in Hindu myth (the Upanishad, Buhad Asinyaka) or, again, in the Empedoclean myth.[16] The recourse to different myths, whose only common feature is the restoration of an initial state, is ample proof of their function; to give the theory a systematic character which goes beyond the clinical evidence, even though Freud, wishing to base his theories on nothing but the results of observation, leaves unanswered the question of whether the life instincts have a compulsion to repetition or not.

Thus he expresses even greater uncertainty about the final theory of the instincts than about his two previous theories:

> These two innovations were a direct translation of observation into theory and were no more open to sources of error than is inevitable in all such cases. It is true that my assertion of the regressive character of instincts also rests upon

> observed material – namely on the facts of the compulsion to repeat. It may be, however, that I have over-estimated their significance. And in any case, it is impossible to pursue an idea of this kind except by repeatedly combining factual material with what is purely speculative (*mit bloss Erdachtem combiniert*) and thus diverging widely from empirical observation ... The more frequently this is done in the course of constructing a theory, the more untrustworthy, as we know, must be the final result. (*Beyond the Pleasure Principle*)[17]

Freud even goes so far as to say that as regards the great problems of science and life, and their ultimate principles, impartiality is impossible: 'Each of us is governed in such cases by deep-rooted internal prejudices into whose hands our speculations unwittingly plays' (ibid.). Thus, by virtue of their common psychological foundation, there would hardly be any difference between myth and science. We can therefore begin to understand why there is no epistemological barrier to using the Empedoclean myth to fill the lacunae of science; we understand the famous formula of the *New Introductory Lectures* which calls the final theory of instincts 'mythological', and the affirmation that all science is mythological in nature: 'The theory of the instincts is so to say our mythology. Instincts are mythical entities, magnificent in their indefiniteness. In our work we cannot for a moment disregard them, yet we are never sure that we are seeing them clearly.'[18]

> As a result of a little speculation,[19] we have come to suppose that this instinct is at work in every living creature and is striving to bring it to ruin and to reduce life to its original condition of inanimate matter. Thus it quite seriously deserves to be called a death instinct ... It may perhaps seem to you as though our theories are a kind of mythology (*eine art von Mythologie*), and, in the present case, not even an agreeable one. But does not every science come in the end to a kind of mythology like this? Cannot the same be said today of your physics? (*Why War?*)

However, the psychological foundation of the ultimate principles of science does not mean that any theory is admissible: one should reject those theories that are contradicted by the most elementary steps in the analysis of observed facts, while at the same time remaining aware that one's own theory can claim no more than a 'provisional validity' and must be abandoned as soon as it is no longer operative. Only believers ask science to replace the catechism.

Hence to make a comparison between Freud and Empedocles is not arbitrary. If Freud shows a particular interest in Empedocles' mythical philosophy it is because, like all myths, it illustrates for Freud a psychic truth. As an illustration it serves as an exemplary model for the final theory of the instincts at the same time as being the proof of its validity. In turn it receives its principle of intelligibility and ultimate foundation from Freud's theory.

On the interest of Empedocles for psychoanalysis

Once the differences between the two theories pointed out by Freud himself have been taken into account, are the two doctrines really identical? At first sight they seem to bear hardly any resemblance to one another. Empedocles' areas of concern are shared by all the presocratic philosophers and his speculative and cultural context is completely different to Freud's. Nevertheless, we must look in some detail at his concerns so as to determine the precise nature of the Freudian thesis of an unconscious truth to the myth.[20]

For Empedocles, as for Parmenides, the One and Being are identical. The One is in existence from the beginning and its reign is that of harmony as opposed to the Anaxagorean notion of an originary chaos. Once this state has come to an end, all that comes to be and the forces which constitute the world of change will tend towards its restoration. The One is thus both origin and end, it is immanent in the world of becoming from which it gradually emerges. Being is being and becoming One. This unity is represented by the image of the sphere. The world is a divine 'sphairos' which, as in Parmenidean doctrine, is homogeneous, uniform, immobile, immortal. The sphere is equal to itself in every direction and it keeps its shape only by virtue of its own circumference. The sphere designates the unity of Being, plenitude, the transcendence of all difference. It has no human form, no limbs, and its roundness indicates that everything in it is ruled by the principle of love. Hate is banished to the circumference.

> There the swift limbs of the sun are not distinguished ... in this way it is held fast in the close covering of harmony, a rounded sphere, rejoicing in encircling stillness, no discord or unseemly warring in the limbs for two branches do not spring from his back, he has no feet, no swift knees, no organs of reproduction, but he is equal to himself in every direction, without any beginning or end, a rounded sphere, rejoicing in encircling stillness. (21, 98, 22)[21]

In the *Katharmoi* (*Purifications*) men have a 'fantasy' of this initial and perfect state of the cosmogony in the mythical form of a golden age, a lost paradise where innocence and harmony reign supreme. This age is said to have come to an end because of an original crime, a crime committed under the influence of hate. Every murder that takes place in the present is a perpetuation and repetition of this primal discord, the cause of all evils, which men must expiate by a quasi-indefinite transmigration of souls. Empedocles presents himself as a fallen god, wandering in exile; blessed with a salvatory power which comes, on the one hand, from his knowledge of the unity of what is (thanks to the numerous metamorphoses he has undergone) and, on the other, from the remedy he proposes, which is an ethic based on love and a democratic, panhellenic political doctrine.

Empedocles is not the first to have written such a *Treatise on Purification*, but his originality lies in the way he unites wisdom and science. His two poems present complementary aspects of his vision of the world. Here, unlike Pythagorianism, the eschatology is transposed from a framework of initiation to one of a knowledge which tries to transmit itself via an explanation of the principle of all things. It could be said that the *Katharmoi* is simply the mythical, sometimes allegorical translation of the *Physics*, which would be its truth.[22]

The different reincarnations are simply the image of the continuous movement which links and unites all that appears discontinuous, an image of the ontological unity of all living things. Knowledge implies an anterior coincidence with what one is referring to – not because there is in reality a transmigration of souls but because man is merely a moment in the continuous play of the elements, the identical roots of all things. There is here, as in all myth, a transposition from a synchronic to a diachronic plane. For the same reasons, what is an ontological principle in the *Physics* is in the *Katharmoi* an ethical principle. In the latter Empedocles' doctrine comes close to Manicheism: love is good, hate evil and the root of all evils, whereas on an ontological level both principles are necessary. His ethical and political doctrines are both the mythical expressions of this ontology and the solutions offered to mankind in order to restore the unity of the sphere of which they are mere fragments.[23]

This unity of the sphere is only one with the love which is found at the centre once the different elements have been reunited. In fact the sphere, which is outside time, nevertheless contains everything that comes into being. On this level the union is so perfect that differentiation between the elements does not exist and consequently they are not distinguishable as such. But it is this originary belonging to the One which founds the ontological unity of the elements and allows them to unite despite their diversity. The name Empedocles gives to this bond between dissimilar elements, a bond which is strong enough to suppress the differences between them, is love. Hate, on the contrary, is the principle of differentiation, and when it dominates, only like is able to unite with like. Life is possible only thanks to the joint intervention of both love and hate. The originality of Empedocles' philosophy is in his realization that a double principle is needed to explain movement.[24] If love were the only principle, the only possibility would be the reign of the sphere, of immobility and identity without differentiation. If only hate existed, then there would be absolute separation – to some extent also the reign of the identical, since in this case only the attraction of similars would be possible.

Certain aspects of this cosmogony could not fail to interest Freud. First of all, the general question of the relationship between the One and the Many would not be unfamiliar, although he would perhaps reverse its formulation: how is the One created from the Many and more precisely from two? Would Freud not see in this common concern of all cosmogonies an unconscious displacement of the sexual problem? Would he not regard Empedocles' poem as a vast symbolic representation of sexual love, as Nietzsche did?[25] The problem of the One and the Many is also present in Freud's own theories when it is a question of instinct and its relation to the partial drives/instincts.

Moreover, the description of the unity and immobility of the sphere and of humanity's nostalgia for a primal golden age is not without echoes of the longing for the mother's breast; of primary narcissism as the 'absolute zero state of excitation'; but also of secondary narcissism as the 'obliteration of the trace of the Other in the desire for Unity, for auto-sufficiency, for immortality, the condition of which is auto-genesis, both death and at the same time the negation of death'.[26]

But there is also an important difference. In Empedocles, love, as the source of perfect union, means the absence of tensions. For Freud, Eros brings about an increase in tension, and narcissism is the culture of death, although Eros is intimately bound up with the death instincts; in this case what is proper to the death instinct is installed in the very heart of love. To use the Empedoclean image again, love is at the centre and hate at the circumference, whilst for Freud, with regard to narcissism, Eros is at the edge and the death instinct at the centre.

Nonetheless, for Empedocles, love is also, in terms of the world of change, the life principle and hate the principle of division and death. This is why it would be an oversimplification to try and invert the two sets of terms. Moreover, even when love is the principle of immobility in the sphere, it is as the harmonizing principle of a multiplicity which is so intimately mixed that all differentiation disappears, whereas the desire for a state of absolute inexcitation calls into play not the principle of stability but that of nirvana: that is, the principle of nullifying reduction.

As in Empedocles there is between the *Physics* and the *Katharmoi* a movement from the ontological to the ethical, so in some of Freud's works there is a shift from the biophysical to the cultural plane. In *Civilisation and its Discontents* and *Why War?*, the death instinct is 'represented' essentially by the instinct of aggression, and Eros, like love in Empedocles' poems, is the salvatory principle of culture. For there are two solutions to the discontents of civilization; the first is the internalization of the aggressive instinct at the expense of individual life, and the second is Eros, which brings men together into ever greater unities. Freud's advice to develop international bodies to work against war is somewhat reminiscent of Empedocles' panhellenism. But in Freud's case, the antagonism between the 'two giants' is insurmountable. Each individual unity to some extent represents a death force for the larger unity, which must of necessity use a certain amount of violence against it. In contrast, in Empedocles every unity formed is a force driving beyond itself towards a superior unity: in effect the nostalgia for the primary unity is present in all forms of life. Moreover, in Freud, as the death instinct always inhibits Eros, perfect unity could never exist, except in fantasy. As well, Freud warns against any form of Manicheism: the death instinct in culture's condition of possibility, so that there is always the need for a close collaboration between the two instincts.

Finally, Empedocles' examples of an original crime could not fail to find favour with Freud, who would be able to see them as further evidence for the Oedipal complex.

Love and strife, Eros and the death instincts

But above all, it is the two fundamental principles of love and hate that Freud declares expressly to be identical 'in form and function'[27] to Eros and the death instincts. Properly speaking the Empedoclean terms are not identical to the names used by Freud: the Greek word Empedocles uses to designate love is never Eros, although he does use a plurality of names: Philotes, Philia, Aphrodite, Harmonia, Kypris, Storge.[28] Hate is never designated by θάνατος, but by νεῖκος, Πόλεμος, Ἔρις, κότος.[29]

Does this plurality not prove that, as in the Freudian theory, love and hate are never directly observable, but are only to be detected through their effects and representatives and that all these derive genetically from the same source, despite their diversity? How do these two forces function? As in Freud, both are necessary and indestructible: from the age of the sphere, and in the world of change, their antagonism is irreducible. Both are immortal principles. At the origin love is at the centre of the sphere and hate at the circumference. 'When its time comes', hate intervenes and the world of change is born. Between the end of the age of the sphere and the beginnings of the world there is a momentary and abstract period in which disorder reigns and everything is still uncompounded. Everything is indeterminate, this time because the whole is totally divided rather than, as previously, because love is dominant. This is the only moment when hate triumphs, when love has not yet rejoined it at the centre of the whirl of elements from which the return begins.

Thus for Empedocles there are only two mythical moments – that of the sphere and that of the origins of the world of change – when one of the two forces triumphs over the other. Similarly, in Freud, the only point at which there could have been a radical separation of the two forces of life and death is in the mythical time of the origin of living beings, even though both forces are present right from the origin. At all other times the two principles are involved in concurrent and mutually opposing action without either emerging as the definitive victor. Complete diffusion only occurs in cases of pathological illness (like melancholia or obsessional neurosis) and at the moment of death.

Love thus appears primarily as a principle which unites dissimilars, and hate a principle of division which brings disorder in the wake of an originary order – the order of the perfect mixture. But hate is not a principle of absolute disorder: it disturbs the unity of the sphere, causing great disasters and storms (in this sense it differs greatly from the silent death instinct) by its opposition to love, but it is by this very action that it provokes the activity of the latter; love intervenes with ever increasing force to restore the order which has been lost. Moreover, if hate is what causes the corruption of the sphere it is also what generates the world of change. It is a positive principle of the differentiation of forms. If it exists even within the sphere itself, at its circumference, it is because without it, to a certain extent, the One itself would lose its form. In the world of change, hate ensures the survival of distinct forms by preventing the One being formed at the expense of living beings: if hate were not in the world, everything would be One. If hate is not, properly speaking, the creator of forms (such creation being the work of love), it is the source of their diversity by its diverse opposition to love.

The present order of the world is maintained thanks to the equilibrium of the two forces. The traditional version of the myth, to which Freud refers, describes the universal process as an endless, uninterrupted alternation of periods of dominance by one or other principle: where first love, then strife gains the upper hand, during which time the defeated force asserts itself and in turn vanquishes its opponent. The continued existence of the world of change is ensured by these alternating struggles and their predetermined outcomes, each one consisting in a movement from absolute submission to absolute dominance. As the two forces contest for control of the four elements, there would be two periods of supremacy towards which things would necessarily tend and two worlds of opposed tendencies, in which both love and hate would be found, but which would differ radically from each other. One would tend irreversibly towards dissolution through union due to a continuing increase of mixtures; the other towards dissolution through separation due to an increasing preponderance of incompatibilities and the dissolution of unions. Thus there would twice be the formation of a world of change under opposing empires.

In the middle of each period, both forces would be in equilibrium; at all other times one or other would dominate. There would thus be four distinct stages, two matching sets of pairs. In fact,[30] Empedocles' expressions 'under love' and 'under hate' are ambiguous: they do not correspond to opposing worlds of change. The oppositions he refers to are, in fact, always those between the world of the sphere and the world of change. When τότε appears in the text, it does not refer to another world of change, but to the sphere. Love's empire extends to the sphere, and throughout the world of change as its power gradually increases. Hate establishes its empire when it destroys the unity of the sphere and inaugurates the cosmogony. But it is necessarily always present in the world of change, because without it there could be no life. Moreover, the four-stages theory would mean the destruction of a world without a return to the origin, a return that the Empedoclean notion of a cycle implies.

Finally, there is nothing in either of Empedocles' poems to support the idea of these successive double formations. Only one universe, our own, is described and only one cycle: the return to the same initial state from which the universe first emerged: 'A twofold tale I shall tell: at one time it grew to be one, only one from many; and at another again it divided to be many from one' (17).[31]

If this is the case, Freud is even closer to Empedocles than he imagined. Firstly, it is clear that the functions of the death instincts and Eros are, in essence, identical to those of hate and love. The death instincts are primarily a principle of the diffusion and separation of the instincts, just as hate is a principle of disjunction, division and rupture. Eros is a factor of fusion, conjunction and coalescence, just as love is a factor of union, fusion, and harmonious combination.[32] In Freudian theory, as in Empedoclean, the opposed instincts work simultaneously. The process of diffusion by which each class of instinct would recover its separate aim is pathological:

> a very extensive fusion and amalgamation of the two classes of instincts takes place, so that we never have to deal with pure life instincts or pure death instincts but only with mixtures of them in different amounts. Corresponding to a fusion of instincts of this kind there may, as a result of certain influences, be a *de*-fusion of them ... This masochism would thus be evidence of, and a remnant from, the phase of development in which the coalescence, which is so important for life, between Eros and the death instincts took place. (*The Economic Problem of Masochism*)[33]

The question, for Freud, is how these two opposing forces can cooperate without, as in the traditional version of Empedocles' myth, one neutralizing the other. Is it a case of the aim of one of them subordinating that of the other according to their respective quantities? In effect, such changes in the proportions of the instincts do appear to have serious consequences: in *An Outline of Psychoanalysis*, Freud notes that: 'A surplus of sexual aggressiveness will turn a lover into a sex murderer, while a sharp diminution in the aggressive factor will make him bashful or impotent'.[34] In

The Ego and the Id he writes that 'the essence of a regression of libido (e.g. from genital to the sadistic-anal phase) lies in a de-fusion of instincts, just as, conversely the advance from the earlier phase to the definitive genital one would be conditioned by an accession of erotic components'.[35] But the quantitative argument cannot provide the solution to the problem because Eros, whatever its quantity may be, is a principle of union and, conversely, the death instincts, even when in a minimal quantity, constitute one of diffusion. This explains why Freud, by declaring that the aim of investigation would be to know how elements of both classes of instinct combine to fulfil the different vital functions, how these combinations are made and broken, states the problem without really managing to resolve it (cf. *Analysis Terminable and Interminable*).

In this collaboration – a collaboration which is necessary for the maintenance of the vital state – do both forces possess equal strength? In Freud's theories Life sometimes appears to be the supreme finality as Eros succeeds in bringing into its service the death instinct, in one form or another. Sexual possession, for example, makes use of sadistic aggression and cultural development of moral masochism. At other times everything seems to be at the service of the death instincts, since life itself tends to revert to an inorganic state and each of its present triumphs means only that the organism is subsequently able to die its own death. As long as there is life, neither class of instinct can triumph to the exclusion of the other: their conflict is irreducible, a necessary, brute fact. This is why, for Freud, the problem of finality is a false one which serves only to disguise the rule of the irreducible necessity of both forces.

In Empedocles, although both forces are necessary, they nevertheless do not appear to be equal. The triumph of love seems to be the ultimate finality, permitting the restoration of the primal sphere, though this final state is never described by Empedocles.

In effect, at the origin, when hate breaks into the sphere, love has fled to the circumference. Hate breaks the bonds uniting the different elements, realizing this difference by making their differences apparent. The elements are what constitute all things and, at death, everything dissolves back into them. To some extent love merges with them and hate is only their difference. They are invariable and eternal so that, properly speaking, there is neither birth nor death. 'Of all mortal things, no one has birth, nor any end in pernicious death' (12).[36]

Death is merely a decomposition in view of an immediate recomposition. In Empedoclean theory there is no real negativity, except in the form of alterity and plurality. The plenitude of Being differs from that of Parmenidean philosophy because it is multiple. Empedocles multiplies being through the plurality of forms it takes, taking up a position midway between Eleatic unity and Anaxagorean infinity. This Empedoclean double permanence – that of the sphere and that of the elements which are simply its continuation in the world of change – could be interpreted in a Freudian perspective as a form of refuge against the necessity of death. Nevertheless, a similar notion occurs in Freud's own writings when he describes the individual as a branch of the immortal species.

The world changes and evolves through the arrangement and combination of elements. Here too it is the numerical relation, the proportion, of the elements which gives rise to difference and to variation. The elements combine by means of pores and by the proportion between the pores. The essential thing is how commensurate their dimensions are: symmetry is more important than actual measurements. The various elements are united by the bond of harmony. Here, the fundamental function of assimilating differences so that bodies may be formed is carried out by love: 'from the combining of water, earth, air and sun come the forms and colours of mortal things which have now arisen, fitted together by Aphrodite. And as they were being mixed, countless types of mortal things poured forth, fitted with all kinds of forms, a wonder to see' (60, 47).[37]

When the elements unite, no fusion occurs in the strict

sense of the word since there can be no transformation. It is rather a matter of a composition or a juxtaposition. Aristotle compares it tò a wall formed by placing bricks side by side or a mosaic in four colours. The construction is held together by proportion. The criterion for ascertaining proportion is pleasure, the criterion for disproportion, pain. All pleasurable sensations result from the contact between elements. pleasure arises when the elements that are lacking are replaced. Pain comes from the rupture of the laws of the compound as elements separate and are torn apart from one another. Lack is at the root of the desire of like for like. But this lack can only be filled thanks to the law of the affinity of similars, a law we could call the very law of the element, and which only has effect because of hate. At the origin, when the power which assimilates differences and permutes the elements has not yet effectively appeared, Chaos reigns, but it is not a reign of absolute disorder. Elements of the same kind are drawn together in one place, escaping strife but at the same time reinforcing its effects, sincc their differences become concentrated. Hate liberates the force of attraction between like elements. In the whirling orbits of the returning sphere, circles of elements are formed. Thus, paradoxically, hate favours the conservation of the elements whereas love tears them from their proper place and forces them to exchange their properties. (On this level love and hate function in a way that is truly analogous to the Freudian instincts.) From the moment when love and hate have exchanged their ways, the elements are divided between the law of their own necessity and the constraints of love:

> For all these – sun and earth and sky and sea – are one with the parts of themselves that have been separated from them and born in mortal things. In the same way, those that are more ready to combine are made similar by Aphrodite, and fell mutual affection. But such as are different from each other in birth and in mixture and in the moulding of their forms are most hostile, quite inexperienced in union, and grieving deeply at their generation in strife, in that they were born in wrath. (25)[38]

The proportion between pores, and the law of attraction of similars, are the essential principles explaining not only the constitution of bodies but also their growth, as well as perception and knowledge.

It is in this manner that each of the senses is connected with an element that moves towards, and recognizes, the same element outside itself. Fire perceives fire, air perceives air. The effluences that bodies give off fit the pores of the senses. These composite effluences unite all the properties of the body, which the sense analyses with the help of its defining element: the pores recognize the effluence commensurate with them. The life of compounds oscillates between preservation and death, due to the entrance and exit of effluences. Here, hate is the basis of knowledge since it alone can tear the parts of the elements from the tissue of their compounds and allow like to rejoin like. But it is also the source of error, since it fosters the belief that a separation of bodies genuinely exists and hence forgetfulness of the primary ontological unity. Conversely, love is necessary since only it can bring about the conjunction of elements in the correct proportions, only love unites what is internal and what is external.

Thus any knowledge is the ontological participation and reciprocal activity of all living things. The slightest sensation reveals the thing itself, and by the combined use of all senses it is possible to apprehend to totality of the world. This common sense, or thought, is constituted by the blood. Beings who know advance the reign of harmony by giving their elements to the things they perceive, and receiving in turn the effluences of the latter. The conditions of possibility of knowledge are, above all, vital: to understand the being of things is to increase one's own vital forces. The art of directing one's thought depends on an art of living. It is necessary to know what proportions are right for each being and to approach them; the limits of development are determined only by the individual constitution. This is why, once again, desire is at the root of a successful exchange between knowing subject and the world.

In Empedocles, therefore, there is in all spheres a close interdependence of the two principal forces, whose only value is derived from their mutual negation. But the two are not equal; love knows a state of perfection and completion whereas strife is reduced to the alteration of love. As long as love has not reestablished its empire, the world of change can exist. The restoration of the sphere would mean the death of all mortal beings, even though it is this future unity which gives the present universe its provisional unity: there is a presence and continuation of the origin which founds return and repetition. Thus love is indeed predominant, at once origin, end, constitutive harmony of bodies in the world of change, and immanent force in the world which drives it towards a state of ever increasing unity and perfection: a state, paradoxically, that means its own destruction.

But the generation of the world of change could not have occurred without a negative force, the Other which is merely the multiplication of the One. The originality of Empedocles' theory in relation to the theories of his predecessors lies in his division of the cause of movement. Both causes have multiple functions. Both can give rise to both movement and stasis. Love produces stasis when it effaces the differences between the elements in the bonds between living bodies. But stasis is produced by hate when it keeps the elements separate through the affinity of similars. Movement comes primarily from hate, which destroys the combinations of elements, but the love which triumphs in the immobility of the One tears the elements from one another to nail them together with dissimilar elements. Nevertheless, Empedocles varies these two kinds of movement by referring to that caused by the action of hate as 'storm' and that generated by love as 'whirl' – a circular motion, the most perfect expression in movement of the immobility and roundness of the sphere.

Therefore it cannot be concluded that love and hate are opposites. They are rather rivals: Empedocles' model is a political one. Both powers are equally divine and incorruptible. Hate is not evil. What is evil in terms of the divine sphere is good in terms of the world of change: the latter owes its creation and continued existence to hate's division of the One. It could be said, to use Freudian terms once again, that hate, essentially negative force, is that 'uncanniness' that disturbs unity, that means that everything is not one; a strangeness that is expressed by Empedocles' location of hate on and at the limit, at the edge of the sphere. It is the very principle of alterity. It makes the One become multiple; Being, from being immobile, become; the immortal become mortal; it makes the closely bound elements separate and the homogeneous sphere diversify into heterogeneous forms.

Should we ascribe the preponderance of love over hate, the tendency of the world of change to move towards the restoration of a primal unity, to a finality?[39] Freud considers it to be one of Empedocles' merits that he substitutes chance for finality, thus becoming one of the earliest forerunners of materialism. Freudian and Empedoclean theories are once again, in this respect, very similar because, in the final analysis, what determines the movement of all things and the advent of all change in Empedocles and what explains the irreducible antagonism of life and death instincts in Freud is necessity, the divine oath (Ἀνάγκη).[40] Indeed, this is precisely neither a reason nor an explanation. In both theories, the two principles do not 'explain' anything since they do not stem from a quantitative hypothesis; they cannot be measured, and the predominance of one force over the other does not result from a difference in size.

Necessity merges with the very nature of things. Understood within the order of necessity, love and hate are inexorably coupled: it is necessity which prevents the irremediable divergence of their courses. Necessity, which has given rise to the disruption of the One, must also bring about its restoration. Necessity implies that exchange and return take place within the confines of a circle. But necessity must not be confused with chance. For Empedocles τυχεῖν signifies happy, successful conjunction. Elements do not come together by chance, as in the Epicurean system. They enter and can only enter into the mould which fits them, and are regulated by proportion. Via each successful conjuction the One is achieved, so that everything appears subject not to the law of necessity but to the finality of love and the unity of the sphere. But this completion of the One can only occur gradually, so that, at a given moment in time, the unities formed are not always well matched, and neither are the forms satisfactory, which gives the impression of an evolution ruled by chance: 'Many creatures with a face, and breasts on both sides were produced, man-faced bulls arose and again bull-headed men [while others] with male and female nature combined and the bodies they had were dark' (52).[41]

The genesis of man, for example, obeys the necessity of the repetition of the same and the law of the affinity of elements. During the course of this genesis, the first act retains an exemplary value. To each of the cosmogonic and embryonic stages of man's evolution there corresponds a species of animal:[42] man both encompasses and is the sum of all of nature's variations. Love has fashioned the definitive types, the models of the limbs and the form of all parts of the animals' bodies, just as it once fashioned all the multiple variations of a single organ: there are no limbs existing today that did not exist formerly. The human sexual act reproduces the first assembling of the limbs, and the union of male and female is a symbol, in the Greek sense of the term, of the reconstitution of a lost unity. Transformations are a result of the search of the organism in pursuit of its equilibrium and the present harmony of the world is due to a succession of necessary events which repeat an already achieved harmony: the myth enables one to explain present structures. The evolution of the species repeats the history of everything always already completed mythically. Thus it passes through four stages marked by an ever greater progression towards unity.

First of all, the parts of the body, separate limbs wandering aimlessly, are formed from the earth. Hate is stronger than love, which does not have sufficient power to impose a union that can sustain life: 'Here many heads sprang up without necks, bare arms were wandering without shoulders, and eyes needing foreheads strayed singly' (50).[43]

Gradually love gains the upper hand and the limbs come together to form monstrous unions. At this point evolution seems to be an effect of chance. In the third stage complementary parts are united. Finally, beings are no longer formed from homogeneous elements but from the combination of dissimilar ones. The condition of possibility for their union is the beauty of the females, creating an excitation in the eye which gives rise to the movement of sperm.[44] Through sexual union, a much richer unity than individual unity is accomplished. Sexual union is a means of going beyond plurality towards unity, and it works towards the restoration of the primal unity of the sphere.

Thus, for Empedocles as for Freud, there is no finality: a necessity reigns which merges into the repetition of the same in difference.

The style of the analogy

One final point seems worthy of consideration and of interest to the psychoanalyst – Empedocles' style, which is reminiscent of the primary processes of the unconscious. The two poems are written in epic meter: Empedocles takes the Iliad as his model in retracing the gesture of the One. The first book of the Iliad begins with the conflict between Achilles and Agamemnon, and the whole poem is an effort to restore the unity which has been lost ('Νεῖκος' is a term which Empedocles borrows from Homer).

In similar fashion the unity of the sphere, disrupted by strife, tends towards restoration in the world of change that follows. The dactylic rhythm expresses the continual progression towards the One which moves through the poem, the spondees set the immobility of the sphere against the movement of change. The opposing rhymes convey the antitheses of the cosmos. The enjambements indicate disruption or violent opposition of strife. The growth of love and the unity of beings is indicated by the absence of cesuras: on occasion six or seven verses must be read continuously. Empedocles' style follows perfectly the very movement of the universe. This is why there are numerous repetitions interspersed with changes, since return always goes hand in hand with difference. It also explains the polysemous and metaphorical character of his language: all designation is arbitary, conventional and partial. Things never let themselves be correctly designated by a single word: words divide beings which, ontologically, are profoundly united.

It is not from a concern for poetic embellishment or to break the monotony that Empedocles uses various terms to designate love (Philotes, Philia, Kypris, Aphrodite, Storgê). His polysemia is a deliberate attempt to abolish the limits set by vocabulary. Metaphor is thus the language best suited to Being. Analogy is the privileged instrument for the restoration of the One: it makes the original affinities apparent. Unity is restored in the condensation of significations metaphor effects. Here, poetry is inseparable from science.

Freud's fantasy

Freud's reading of the Empedoclean cosmogony, which confers upon it a paradigmatic status and transforms it into the proof of his final theory of the instincts, presupposes a kernel of analytic truth at work within the myth: Empedocles had an obscure, endopsychic knowledge of the unconscious and its laws. Freud's reading itself seems to be motivated by nostalgia for a primal unity, by the seductiveness of an analogy between past and present, poetry and psychoanalysis. Bridging the rupture and the gulf created by Socrates (an 'excessively logical spirit', a 'man of theory'[45] *par excellence*, according to Nietzsche), Freud renews the link with the presocratic tradition. By privileging myth over science, by repeatedly affirming his own lack of originality and by showing himslf to be fascinated and amazed by the genius of Empedocles, he brings to an end the ostracism of the presocratics by science and metaphysics, which traditionally characterized them as uninteresting by virtue of being more poets than philosophers. A gesture by Freud which brings him closer to Nietzsche than to Aristotle or Hegel. But his gesture is ambiguous: to assert that the Empedoclean and psychoanalytic visions are identical – or almost identical – is to efface the differences which exist between them to try to take from Empedocles what cannot be taken from him, to strip his poems of their beauty by enlisting them in the service of the analytic cause. Are not Freud's repeated declarations of indifference to questions of priority and originality simply, in fact, so many negations which serve to conceal his fantasy of mastering his predecessors? A fantasy which concurs with the fantasy of the whole of western metaphysics since Aristotle.

A gesture of mastery which, according to Nietzsche, is idiosyncratic of philosophers and which he tries to evaluate genealogically by turning the question of the relationship between art and philosophy on its head. Far from asking what aspect of truth is to be found disguised within a myth or poem, he asks to what extent philosophy itself cannot be considered to be, in fact, a work of art; and what can remain of it when, scientifically, it is a dead system; when it can no longer be reinscribed into the process of some truth or other. It is only by paying attention to this (remainder) and to its artistic character that the instinct for knowledge can, in turn, be mastered.[46] Thus one begins to understand why it is essential, in terms of the need of psychoanalysis and philosophy (but can we, from a genealogical point of view, continue to make a distinction between them?) for mastery, to dismiss this remainder as negligible, 'oriental', childish, as something which makes a game of the seriousness of reason and work, something that is to be '*relevé*'[47] in the course of the development of the truth.

One perhaps begins to understand more clearly why Freud took so much trouble to avoid reading Nietzsche . . .

Judith

[The theme of the ring] leaves one once again with the impression of how hard it is for a psychoanalyst to discover anything new that has not been known before by some creative writer.

Freud, *The Psychopathology of Everyday Life*

Judith

The taboo of virginity

The Taboo of Virginity[1] proposes to solve the mystery of the strange evaluation primitive peoples make of virginity. For such peoples, defloration is the subject of a taboo and the consecration of the hymen is performed outside marriage. A paradox for our civilizations, where it is a matter of honour for a husband to deflower his wife and where defloration leads to a state of sexual subjugation – the basis of monogamy in civilized societies.

Psychoanalysis, however, can provide a justification for what appears at first sight to be a matter of mere prejudice. To solve the mystery Freud follows a chain of argument that is reminiscent of free association. His line of reasoning seems disordered: facts from different civilizations, from religious rites and other customs, the phenomena of normal or pathological mental life, dreams and neurotic symptoms, missionaries' and natives' accounts, and, finally, literary texts of different genres – short story, comedy, tragedy – are all cited as evidence. His approach seems to mimic that of the patient on the couch. On the occasion of a dream the patient evokes childhood memories, other dreams, a jumbled mixture of mental and cultural phenomena. He brings the whole of his experience to bear by erasing differences and masking the heterogeneity of the material by the homogeneity of the function it fulfils. The different elements are merely the fragments of a future, hypothetical construction, each one throwing light upon another, in a circular fashion.[2] Thus what occurs spontaneously during analysis is elevated into a method by Freud. His premise is that there is no essential difference in kind between a psychic text and a cultural text: the same unconscious processes are at work in both. Thus both types of text are treated on some occasions as enigmatic, as symptomatic, to be deciphered, and on others as tools in a method which is to be used to decipher other texts.

This intertextual and circular method is justified only by its efficacy on the level of the cure and by its operative character. It is a method which, more than any other, makes the text intelligible in its totality, right down to its most 'insignificant' details. Only this method can explain why a certain symptom is expressed by a certain symbol. The recourse to philology, folklore, mythology, ritual and art[3] reveals a system of symbols that is common to all cultural and psychic productions: they are all so many dialects of the unconscious which echo one another.[4] Such a method brings to light an unsuspected unity between heterogeneous phenomena: a unity which calls for an interdisciplinary approach.[5] Investigations by a specialist in one particular field are doomed to failure and can only help to keep mankind in a state of metaphysical illusion.

In *The Taboo of Virginity*, the disorder of the Freudian discourse is *strategic*; it erases the oppositions, the hierarchical distinctions between different mental faculties and between people which lead to the privileging of the normal over the pathological, the civilized over the primitive etc. It is also *methodical*: through this disorder, Freud hopes to construct a primal configuration which repeats itself, and which is masked by the heterogeneity of different texts. As originary substitutes for an invariable that never reveals itself, Freud does not put all these texts on the same footing: community of function is not incompatible with structural differences. The 'echo' is always a 'caricature' of what it repeats.[6] The striking concordances between texts do not cancel out the dissonances. It is these dissonances that the order of Freud's argument takes into account, an order which free association itself merely caricatures. The fact that Freud begins his investigation with an appeal to expert opinion and ends it with a reference to literary texts from different 'genres' is not due to chance nor the result of the incompetence of a mere 'layman'.[7] A rigorous method is at work, a method which moves from the most superficial to the most profound, the most repressed to the least repressed, from the most general to the most specific.

But why does Freud privilege the literary text in such a way? By giving the text the status of the proof at the heart of an experimental method, is one not ignoring its specificity, confusing 'beauty' and 'truth', art and science? Freud's use of the literary text as confirmation of the validity of his argument does not, however, exclude him from according it a certain autonomy, as is illustrated by the place he assigns to it in his argument. Conversely, to refuse to 'apply' the analytic method to literature, in order to preserve, at any cost, its specificity, is to give literature a sacred character, and to reinstate the system of metaphysical oppositions Freud has scotched. It seems to me that what Freud does is to establish a genetic relation between different productions and at the same time to maintain their irreducibility on a structural level.[8] This should be obvious to anyone who examines the order of his argument.

Freud begins with a summary of the information provided by the specialists. Krafft-Ebing traces the formation of sexual subjection back to the coincidence between 'an uncommon degree of the state of being in love and of weakness in character' in one person, and 'unbounded egoism' in another. Analytic experience shows the unsatisfactory nature of 'this simple attempt at explanation'. Crawley provides numerous facts but regrettably fails to distinguish between the simple rupture of the hymen without coitus and coitus for the purpose of perforating the hymen. As for the data supplied by Bartels-Ploss, it is practically useless (despite being in some respects extremely productive). The anatomical data and the author's descriptions of it serve as an anti-cathexis to the psychological importance of the act of defloration, which is not discussed.

If Freud avails himself, first of all, of the opinion of 'experts', it is only to eliminate their evidence as quickly as possible: no text can be objective, as all perception is pre-invested with desire and every eye censors as it sees. Description is already interpretation: 'The authors to whom I have had access either have been too embarrassed to discuss the matter or have once again underestimated the psychological importance of such sexual details.'

'Objectivity' is dangerous because the secondary rationalizations which cover over the lacunae in knowledge pass for truths. Travellers' or missionaries' accounts would have been a richer source of information. Every attempt at explanation which makes an economy in the analytical process is necessarily partial, in both senses of the word, and turns a specific case into a more general one. Thus some explanations take into account the loss of blood that takes place during a defloration but reduce the taboo of virginity to a specific instance of the taboo of blood. The specifically sexual nature of the former is thus repressed and it becomes related solely to the prohibition against murder. Other explanations reduce the taboo of virginity to the taboo of menstruation, which for primitive peoples carries sadistic connotations. The fact goes unnoticed that in certain cases specifically connected with sexuality, like circumcision or clitoral excision, the taboo of blood no longer operates.

Elsewhere, the suggestion is found that primitive peoples are of an anxious disposition which makes itself particularly manifest on occasions in which something unexpected occurs. The taboo of virginity in this case would relate to the 'anxiety of new beginnings'. Once again, in this explanation, the specifically sexual nature of the taboo is repressed. Even when certain accounts do finally mention sexuality, it is in its most general sense: the taboo of virginity is explained as a particular case of the taboo of sexual intercourse, which can be explained by the fear that woman provokes as the Other *par excellence*. Such a generalization 'throws no light on the particular rules concerning the first sexual act'.

Freud focuses on the specificity of the taboo by lifting the repression that operates on it. '*Denying or sparing precisely the future husband something*' seems to be the taboo of virginity's proper function. To avoid becoming sidetracked in his turn by generalities, Freud immediately excludes the use of a generic method which would trace the specific taboo of virginity back to the origin of taboo observances in general. The search for an origin would condemn his investigation to failure: the 'primitive', the 'originary' do not exist; they are always already covered over by subsequent layers of signification. They cannot be used as a point of departure because they are the end result of a construction. Taboos are texts whose sense has already been distorted by numerous displacements, a sense already corrupted by rationalizations: 'Today we find taboos ... already elaborated into an intricate system of just the sort that neurotics ... develop in their phobias.'

Thus the taboo of virginity resembles the manifest text of a dream; its latent sense must be constructed using other texts which have themselves been falsified. It is a question of deducing from the new motifs the 'archaic motifs' that are disguised in a different form in other texts and other contexts. Every text is merely a differential variation of a common core which is at play within its distorted form; an abbreviated version of a single, originary text. One begins to understand why data from different civilizations, from normal or pathological mental life, can be used to read these texts.

Thus the behaviour of civilized women, who often experience disappointment after the first act of intercourse, is the point of departure for Freud's investigation. But taking normal, civilized women as a starting point is not the result of chance or ethnocentricity. In view of Freud's premise that 'instinctual repression' is 'a measure of the level of civilisation',[9] the most repressed, rationalized and superficial behaviour is to be found in normal, civilized people. As in the cure, where the surface layers of the psyche must be deconstructed, by gradually and progressively breaking down the patients' resistances, in order to reach the deepest levels, so Freud begins with the most obvious, most transformed texts and moves towards those texts that are the most profound and least distorted. Closest to the originary text would be the pathological, the primitive, the artistic. A paradox in terms of usual modes of thought: the less rational a text appears to be, the more it explains, just as those details which are apparently the most insignificant are the most revealing. An analytic method of deconstruction which parodies that of Descartes or Durkheim.

With this in mind it is obvious why the behaviour of normal, civilized women can be elucidated by pathological cases which 'throw light' on 'the riddle of female frigidity'. What such cases reveal is that 'the danger which is ... aroused through the defloration of a woman' consists of incurring the hostility which defloration unleashes in her. This hostility does not stem from the pain involved in defloration but seems rather to stem from the narcissistic injury involved in the destruction of an organ. This explanation does not, however, touch the heart of the matter, as is made evident by a detail from the marriage customs of primitive peoples. The ceremony usually falls into two distinct phases: 'After the hymen has been ruptured (by hand or with some intrument) there follows a ceremonial act of coitus or mock-intercourse with the representatives of the husband.' Thus the idea that the disappointment experienced after the first coitus stems from the discrepancy between 'fulfilment' and 'expectation' does not go far enough and could only apply in the case of civilized women.

These last two pieces of evidence, which are apparently unconnected, find their common explanation in the history of libidinal development. What we learn from the latter is that her father is a girl's first love-object: her husband is always merely a substitute. The customs of primitive peoples take into account this motif of an early sexual wish, just as the civilized woman's disappointment is symptomatic of an intense father fixation. Freud then gathers together the evidence for such an hypothesis: the *jus primae noctis* of the medieval lord, the tradition of '*Tobias Nights*', the sacrifice of the hymen to the symbol or statue of the gods in India or in the Roman marriage ceremony. Despite its universality, this new explanation still fails to penetrate the deepest layers of the psyche. The 'archaeologist' has only reached the stage of first object-choice.

The first act of coitus activates even deeper and more primitive drives, those that run counter to the feminine role and function. This is illustrated by the penis envy manifested by neurotic women, an envy which, at the stage of object-choice, is replaced by the desire for a child: 'the masculine phase in the girl in which she envies the boy for his penis is (in any case) developmentally the earlier, and it is closer to the original narcissism than it is to object love.' Penis envy is connected with the castration complex. The proof? Certain details from the dream of a newly married woman which show her desire to castrate her husband and keep his penis for herself: 'Behind this envy for the penis, there comes to light the woman's hostile bitterness towards the man, which never completely disappears in the relations between the sexes, and which is clearly indicated in the strivings and in the literary productions of the "emancipated women".'

With the discovery of the castration complex, the mystery of the taboo of virginity is solved: 'the womans's *immature sexuality*[10] is discharged onto the man who first makes her acquainted with the sexual act. This being so, the taboo of virginity is reasonable enough.' As analytic practice shows, it is impossible to go beyond this discovery: 'We have often the impression that, with the wish for a penis and the masculine protest, we have penetrated through all the psychological strata and have reached bedrock, and thus all our activities are at an end.'[11]

The Judith 'theme'

Thus at this point Freud could have concluded his analysis. However, he does not: the analysis continues and ends with a reference to three literary texts which prove the survival of the taboo of virginity in modern civilization and confirm the various hypotheses. While the expert presents a lacunal text as if it were the truth, the writer reveals the truth as illusion and through illusion:[12] he or she 'plays' or 'acts' knowledge without possessing it, 'depicts' it, dramatizes it: 'The taboo of virginity has been depicted (*Darstellung*) most powerfully of all in a well-known dramatic character, that of Judith in Hebbel's tragedy.' The writer, with 'the fine perception of a poet . . . sensed the ancient motive, which had been lost in the tendentious narrative [of the Old Testament]'. An endopsychic perception which is the privilege of artists, of superstitious and primitive peoples and also of certain psychotics. A knowledge which is always expressed indirectly, projected into a work of art, a myth, a paranoid delusion: a knowledge which is always displaced and distorted by its projection from the interior to the exterior; a knowledge 'which, of course, has nothing of the character of a [true] recognition'.[13]

What is projected into the external world bears witness to what has been erased from consciousness. This means that the literary text can only 'depict' the taboo of virginity if one also allows this text itself to be subjected to an analytic interpretation. Holofernes' decapitation is only a symbolic substitute for castration in the eyes of someone who already accepts the symbolism of dreams. If a work of art is regarded as the projection of relationships which the writer has repressed, then the singularity of each dramatization finds its explanation in the parental complex of each author. Thus in addition to his comparative method, Freud uses a generic method which allows him to grasp the differences which exist over and above the repetitions of a single theme.

But what does it mean to say that the same theme can be

treated in different literary genres? What is a theme? Is it the nature of the material, its richness, that allows it to be treated in diverse ways? And is a particular genre best suited to a particular subject matter?

Thus sexual subjection of men or women explains 'not a few tragic events',[14] but comic situations can also arise from the contrast between the raising of the prohibition on intercourse in marriage and the taboo nature of virginity (p. 206).

Nevertheless, according to *The Uncanny*,[15] that work of Freud's which perhaps more than any other takes into account the specificity of literature, the writer's privilege is the ability to produce a great variety of effects from the same material: in the world of fiction, the effect obtained is independent of the subject matter chosen. The author is not restricted by reality-testing, which means that he or she has a greatly enlarged range of possibilities. The multiplicity of genres is the expression of literature's independence in relation to life. There is no theme in itself which is then taken up secondarily by literature. The theme is the correlative of a certain kind of writing which depends on the choice made by the author. But this is not a free choice; it is the effect of an internal determination more constraining than reality-testing. Poetic licence is only the other face of an instinctual necessity. It therefore becomes possible both to recognize literature's specificity and at the same time to show its dependency with respect to psychic processes.

The reference, at the end of *The Taboo of Virginity*, to a comedy, Anzengruber's *Virgin's Venom*, to a short story, Schnitzler's *The Fate of Freiherr von Leipenborge*, and to a tragedy, Hebbel's *Judith and Holofernes*, reveals both the identity of the fantasy that is structured in the three texts and the originality of each interpretation. It could be said that the 'theme' of the taboo of virginity only exists in its type as constituted by a certain reading. There is no single figure of Judith prior to the textual treatment of Judith, no original text which would act as a reference for the truth of all possible Judiths. There are as many Judiths possible as there are ways for man to live the Oedipus complex. The text's dramatization harks back to the primal scene, always already repressed, which it plays out, transformed by anxiety or derision into a tragedy or a comedy.

The biblical Judith

What, then, of the biblical Judith? Is she not this reference text, the measure of all other Judiths? In fact the biblical text is even less 'truthful' than Hebbel's play. It consists of numerous contradictory versions, symptomatic of a process of repression.[16] In the Bible, the sexual meaning of the story has been disguised. Judith is able to boast that she has not been defiled and no allusion is made to her bizarre wedding night with Manasses. Hebbel has deliberately sexualized the apocryphal narrative and 'restored its early content to the material', just as Freud himself restores the complete meaning of the taboo of virginity, from behind all the falsifying interpretations of it. Hebbel's text thus contains the truth of the biblical story just as Freud's text makes Hebbel's play decipherable.[17]

If one sticks to the letter of the biblical text, Judith's story seems to illustrate a moral vision of historical events: morality and innocence triumph over force. Defeats are trials sent by God to try the just. The downfall of Holofernes, a previously undefeated general, double of the all-powerful Nabuchodonsor, makes the power of God shine forth even more greatly since it is the result of a ruse conceived and carried out by a mere woman. The numerous references to Judith's beauty only emphasize the means by which the ruse succeeds. Judith is simply an instrument in the hands of God and, as her name indicates, she is identified with the whole Jewish race. After beheading Holofernes she asks for his head to be displayed on the ramparts of the city, because it belongs to all her people. Judith's piety and chastity are signs that she has been specially chosen by God. There seems to be absolutely no psychological motive behind her action.

However, a few details seem to hint at a repressed sexual motive: the Bible gives several versions of the night Judith spends with Holofernes. All these versions emphasize, by way of negation, that she emerges from the affair 'without shame or dishonour'. Another revealing detail is that she beheads Holofernes while he is asleep and, in order to do so, she seizes him by the hair. Her action is reminiscent of Delilah cutting off Samson's hair, Jael driving a peg from the tent in which he had taken refuge into Sisera's head: both women, once again, act whilst their victim is asleep. As sleep generally follows coitus, even if in the Bible it is referred to as the effect of drunkenness, there is an implication that in all three cases the act committed is indeed the symbolic equivalent of castration: 'Woman is different from man, strange and therefore apparently hostile. The man is afraid of being weakened by the woman, infected with her femininity and of then showing himself incapable. The effect which coitus has of discharging tensions and causing flaccidity may be the prototype of what the man fears.'[18]

Moreover, when Judith goes to Holofernes she 'puts off the garments of widowhood'. The Vulgate hastens to clarify this point by assuring us that her show of finery is inspired not by sensuality but by courage. Finally, even in the biblical version, it is possible to uncover a link between Holofernes' decapitation and the taboo of virginity. When the Hebrews recite the various crimes committed by the Assyrians, they list, without making any particular distinction between them, the abduction of women, the massacre of children, the destruction of towns and fields, the theft of flocks. Judith, in the two prayers she addresses to God, singles out the rape of virgins and indicates that in taking their part she is merely following her father Simeon's example. It is this particular bond with her father that perhaps explains why Judith's conception of God contrasts strongly with that of the rest of the Jews. The latter's relation to God is purely mercantile; they put him to the test, ask him for guarantees, and impose time limits upon him. Judith asks them to place an absolute trust in God: his omnipotence means that he can intervene as he sees fit; men must merely humble themselves and bow down before his omnipotence.

Finally, if Judith can be identified with her whole race, it is because, as a woman, she is best able to feel its humiliation. Thus not only does her victory over Holofernes reenact David's defeat of Goliath but also, despite the repression at work in the story, it is possible to see her action as motivated by originary narcissism and a fixation on the first love-object.

Hebbel's Judith

Hebbel's play, according to Freud, sexualizes the story more clearly. However, the author's own account of the motives behind the changes he makes to the biblical story differs from Sadger's account (in an analysis Freud calls excellent).[19] The divergence between the two accounts would be explained by the fact that the author's declared intentions are always a facade designed to conceal what he himself is not conscious of.[20]

Hebbel indicates in a letter that the biblical story is only a pretext for him, and that he does not have the slightest intention of reconstructing an historical fact: 'The fact that one day a treacherous woman beheads a hero is immaterial to me and, indeed, in the form the story takes in the Bible, it leaves me feeling indignant.'[21] This indignation leads him to transform Judith into a virgin-widow. He gives a lengthy explanation of his reasons. The main one is that the biblical Judith would be absolutely implausible in a drama. It would be highly unrealistic for her to consent to the sacrifice in the knowledge of what it will cost; just as it would run contrary to a virgin's naivety to be able ever to contemplate such an act. Judith must therefore both be married and yet remain untouched by her husband. Consequently, Manasses must have been prevented from approaching her on their wedding night.

> Whatever this apparition may be – and this is the secret – it makes no difference. Let everyone think what they will, be it a vision, a ghost – or whatever, it does not matter. The only thing that matters is the consequence of this apparition. The dramatic motivation of her later heroic deed is determined by the unconsummated marriage [*die ehelose Ehe*] that precedes it.[22]

It would have been easy to find a rational explanation for Manasses' impotence. 'Let everyone think what they will' seems to be, as Sadger points out, a disavowal that is revealing of the author's unconscious. Is the fact that Hebbel himself speaks of a secret not an invitation for us, if not to delve into his own unconscious, then at least to solve the mystery of Manasses' impotence? In fact, the play itself offers enough clues to the meaning of the 'secret', and we can only echo Hebbel's own astonishment at the curiosity aroused by this famous 'apparition'.[23] It is of the utmost importance to note the close link Hebbel himself establishes between the wedding night and the decapitation of Holofernes; one conditions the other. What is also known is that Hebbel wrote the fifth act of the play first. He recounts the episode in which, when he was about to embark on a career in law, he came to write his first play and how, at the same time, he found the Judith theme so compelling: 'I had shortly before seen a painting which depicted Judith holding Holofernes' head. It left me with such a powerful impression that I did not need to look for any subject matter, since the theme of Judith imposed itself on me of its own accord. The fifth act, the decisive catastrophe, was completed in a night.'[24]

If we remember that 'each portion which returns from oblivion asserts itself with peculiar force',[25] we can suppose that while he was looking at the painting something from Hebbel's past returned, producing an affect which was then discharged in a dramatic 'creation':[26] Likewise Manasses' paralysis in the face of a strange vision must be connected to a return of the repressed. Perhaps we can go even further and assert that what made an impression on both Hebbel and Manasses was the same; or at least provoked a return of the same affect: the fear of castration.

To Judith, Manasses' sudden paralysis seems uncanny (*Mir ward's unheimlich*). In an obscure way, she understands that her husband's impotence has an unconscious cause: 'Thus we lived side by side. We felt that we belonged to each other, but something seemed to stand between us, something dark, unknown' (*Judith and Holofernes*, Act II, p. 268).[27]

Uncanny effects always stem from a return of some repressed content, even if it is travestied in the form of a spectre or a phantom. Here, Hebbel's 'genius' lies in his ability to construct a text which condenses several possible interpretations, a compromise formation between conscious and unconscious significations. The context of the wedding night allows us to guess that the object that intervenes between Judith and Manasses and that arouses the fear of castration is the mother. Everything points to the conclusion that Manasses has identified Judith with his mother, just as Judith herself identifies with her own dead mother. In this case, his impotence would stem from the fear of incest which lies behind the anxiety caused by the sight of the female genitals: one of its consequences is the fear of castration. Manasses' mental 'paralysis' is analagous to the paralysing effect of the Medusa.[28] The wedding night scene is a form of dress rehearsal for the decapitation scene. Judith's hostility towards Holofernes is all the more violent given that she has been unable to discharge her hate for Manasses effectively and has turned it in upon herself. Thus Hebbel's *Judith and Holofernes* can be seen as a perfect illustration of the hostile reaction the loss of virginity unleashes in women. The 'power' of Hebbel's dramatization lies in the fact that he has condensed into a single work all the different motifs uncovered by Freud on the basis of isolated fragments of evidence. In Hebbel's drama a link is woven between the woman's hostility and father fixation, narcissism of minor differences and penis envy.

If the wedding night is the dramatic preparation for the night Judith spends with Holofernes, it is because, in psychological terms, the final act is a repetition of what is related in the second. The future is always already announced by the past, the compulsion to repeat plays the role of destiny in the tragedy. As soon as Judith appears, she recounts a dream to which she gives the sense of a premonition:

> When men lie in slumber, relaxed, no longer bound by the consciousness of themselves, a sense of the future displaces all the thoughts and images of the present, and the things which come glide like shadows through the soul, preparing, warning, consoling. Thus it happens that the truth so seldom or never takes us unawares, that we hope so confidently for good long before it comes and forbode, though unwittingly, every ill. (*Judith and Holofernes*, Act II, p. 266)

When, in the final act, she beheads Holofernes, Judith experiences a feeling of '*fausse reconnaissance*': 'And woe, woe again! I feel that I thought of that before' (Act V, p. 315).

In her dream, ideas and affects are at work that can foretell the future because they are already a repetition the past. Judith's dream is an anxiety dream: she feels herself compelled to ascend a steep path without knowing where it leads, and experiences a sense of guilt. Having arrived at a certain point, she is unable to go either forwards or backwards and finds herself on the edge of a precipice. The dream expresses metaphorically an instinctual conflict: the ascent towards the heights, towards a mountain bathed in sunlight, expresses the aspirations of the superego and the descent into the abyss the desires of the id. The dream also points to the fact that Judith's sexual desire can only find satisfaction by means of an anti-cathexis; it must take the form of a religious motivation.[29] Hebbel seems to have 'known' that the repressed returns in the very agent of repression itself: in order to find satisfaction, Judith must transform her sensuality into duty, and devote her beauty to God's service. At the edge of the precipice she calls on God to help her and it is from the abyss itself that she hears a 'gentle, sweet' voice call to her. She springs towards it and feels 'unspeakably happy'. But she is too heavy, she falls through the arms that are supporting her and weeps: the satisfaction of desire with the father or his substitute can only be fatal.

The rest of the play elaborates what the dream expresses in a condensed form. In the third act Judith, having fasted for three days, realizes that 'the way to ... [her] deed leads through sin' and that God has the power to transform impure actions into pure ones. But she is not deceived by her own rationalizations: she knows that the religious motivation for her act conceals a sexual and narcissistic motivation. Her joy at seeing Ephraim refuse to go and kill Holofernes is proof of this, as is her fear that 'the Elder' will offer himself as a sacrifice. The presence of a real hero would make her own existence superfluous. Only a heroic action can make her the equal, if not the superior, of all men, which is what she desires above all. The ambiguous meaning of her piety does not escape her either. She must pray as she 'must breathe', if she is 'not to stifle'. She 'plunges into God' as into an abyss, to fight her own fantasies and at the same time to search for a solution to her conflicts. Prayer is for her both a means of being dead to her desire, committing suicide by identifying with her dead mother, and at the same time of being reborn thanks to the paternal support she discovers in it: 'God! God! I feel I must clutch you by the hem of your garment, as one who threatens to forsake me forever!' (Act III, P. 274).

'Therefore am I called pious and God fearing ... If I do that, it is because I no longer know how to save myself from my thoughts. My prayer is then a plunge into God, it is only another form of suicide. I spring into the infinite as desperate men into deep water' (Act II, p. 269).[30]

The instinctual conflict which finds expression in her dream and which is one of the keys to Judith's behaviour plays a decisive role in her wedding night with Manasses. It manifests itself in the close identity she repeatedly establishes between sexuality, death and madness; it is translated into an emotional ambivalence: in the dream, in the scene with Manasses and when she decapitates Holofernes, she feels joy and anxiety simultaneously. Her anxiety could be interpreted as a consequence of Manasses' impotence. Hence, on the wedding night, she seems to find temporary relief through a discharge of tears and laughter, a substitute for the coitus that has not taken place.[31] But it also stems from guilt. Without knowing why, she feels guilty for the failure of her wedding night: 'My beauty is that of the deadly nightshade: Enjoyment of it brings madness and death.' Madness and death for which she appeals in vain after she has submitted to her 'murder'. In vain, because she is too lucid: 'I beg for madness even, and it grows, now and then, gloomy within me, but not dark. In my head are a thousand holes, but they are too small for my great, thick understanding; it seeks in vain to creep in' (Act V, p. 318).

However, even before she sees Manasses she is already overwhelmed by contradictory emotions: every step she takes toward him makes her feel more and more uneasy. 'Now I thought I should cease to live; again, that I was just beginning to live' (Act II, p. 267). Perhaps the shame and anxiety she feels at the onset of desire are caused less by her youth than by the accompanying presence of her father. She cannot help comparing him with her future husband: 'My father walked beside me. He was very solemn and spoke much that I did not hear. At times I looked up at him and then I thought: "Surely Manasses will not be like him"' (ibid.). Here the Oedipal fixation is rekindled and it accounts for the awakening of guilt in Judith: when she sees Manasses' mother she feels immediately hostile towards her.

She justifies this by the fact that she feels she is committing sacrilege in calling her 'mother'. Her explanation must be regarded as a rationalization. In fact, her hostility seems to stem from her projection onto Manasses' mother of the feelings she must have had towards her own mother, who robbed her of her father's presence, just as Manasses' mother always already stands between Judith and her husband. During the wedding night the mother spies on the couple, just as Judith herself must have spied upon her parents. Manasses and his mother form a couple in close league against her: 'His mother scrutinized me, gloomy and scornful. I perceived that she had listened. She said not a word to me and walked, whispering with her son, into a corner' (Act II, p. 268).

Judith's identification of Manasses' mother with her own dead mother explains the ambivalence of her feelings and why she experiences the wedding ceremony as if it were a funeral. If Manasses, on coming face to face with Judith, experiences the fear of castration, she herself explains his impotence as a result of revenge taken on her by her mother, returned from the grave to punish her: 'it seemed as if the black earth had thrust out a hand and clutched him with it' (ibid.). Mother, woman, death: 'they are the three forms taken by the figure of the mother in the course of a man's life – the mother herself, the beloved, who is chosen after her pattern, and lastly the Mother Earth who receives him once more'.[32] Hebbel seems to have condensed the three successive relationships a man has with a woman into a single moment. Even if Manasses had not been impotent, it can easily be assumed that Judith would not have been satisfied and would have decapitated him – symbolically at least. Each of the glances her husband subsequently bestows on her seems like a poisoned arrow against which she can only defend herself by killing him: 'At times, his eyes would rest upon me with an expression that made me shudder. In such moments I could have strangled him, out of terror, in self-defence' (Act II, p. 268).

But Judith's behaviour cannot be explained solely in

terms of disappointment or father fixation. The principal motivation for her action seems indeed to be penis envy, which according to Freud lies behind, in fact, the taboo of virginity. None of these motifs are exclusive of the others: they are complementary. Judith's feelings after the failure of her wedding night can certainly be explained in terms of disappointment:

> A virgin is a silly being who trembles at her own dreams, because a dream can wound her mortally, and who yet lives only by the hope that she will not always remain a virgin. For a virgin there is no greater moment than when she ceases to be one and every bound of her pulse which she subdued before, every sigh which she has repressed, exalts the worth of the sacrifice which she has to offer in that moment. She offers her all – is it too haughty a demand if she wishes to inspire, along with all that, ecstasy and bliss? (Act V, p. 311)

But why should disappointment provoke feelings of self-hatred, shame and the impression of having been defiled? These feelings can only be understood 'after the event': Judith experiences the same feelings after being deflowered by Holofernes; on this occasion she repeats the same words – shame, defilement, degradation, humiliation. In neither case can she accept that the condition of woman is shame and nothingness. Whether she loses her virginity or not, she experiences the same sense of narcissistic injury, quite simply because she is nothing more than a woman – that is a mutilated, incomplete and impure being who is defiled because she is incomplete. Manasses' impotence is experienced as an insult, a manifest refusal to accept her offering. She then fells superfluous, useless because she is nothing or treated as nothing. In Holofernes' arms she feels herself grow weak, lose all self-control. With the loss of her virginity, her whole being founders and she becomes aware of her unbearable dependence on her own body: 'When sleeping desire borrows from your own lips as much fire as it needs to commit murder of the thing most sacred to you – when even your senses, made drunk like slaves who no longer recognise their lord, rise against you' (Act V, p. 311).

If Judith is filled with self-hatred it is because, bodily integrity being denied her, she can only love herself in another, in the man who completes her; in the child, her substitute penis. To her servant, Mirza, who tries to dissuade her from suicide by appealing to her narcissism ('In such a moment you should step before a mirror', p. 269), she replies:

> Foolish! Do you know the fruit that can feed upon itself? Better not to be young and fair than to be so for yourself alone. A woman is nothing; through a man only can she become something; through him she can become a mother. The child that she bears is the only thanks she can offer nature for her existence. Unblessed are the unfruitful; doubly unblessed am I, not a maid, nor a wife! (Act II, p. 269)

Judith hates Manasses because he has denied her the substitute penis that could have made her whole: Manasses, whose impotence is the manifest sign of the danger that the female sex represents to man. Manasses, when he is on the verge of dying, accuses Judith of being the cause of his 'madness' without, however, revealing the key to the mystery which Judith has tried in vain to wring from him. A further injury to her narcissism, since by dying in this way, Manasses robs her of part of her being: 'I felt that he would steal away something from my innermost self' (Act II). The mystery is in fact the riddle of femininity and its solution – penis envy.

That a child is the only satisfactory substitute for the missing penis is made explicit on several occasions: 'We bear children so that we may have a double self, so that we may be able to love that self in the child when it laughs at us so pure and innocent, when we must hate and despise that self in ourselves' (Act V, p. 316). So says a mother, perhaps the same one who ends up devouring her child because she is starving, thus realizing in actuality what until then she has done only symbolically.[33] It is this rapacious, devouring relationship of the mother to the child that explains the fear of castration.

Judith's tragic destiny is that she could only be fulfilled by a child, and that this is always denied her, either because of her husband's impotence or because she herself rejects it: to bear Holofernes' child could only lead to her death. This is the price she demands of the Hebrews by way of reward. At the end of the play she asks God to make her sterile: her fear of bearing Holofernes' child is overdetermined. Sons resemble their fathers; what for others would be an image of purity and integrity would for her be a constant reminder of her sexual 'murder'. Moreover, to be pregnant by Holofernes would be the sign that her action, carried out under the guise of patriotic and religious motives, had nothing supernatural about it and in no way marks her as God's chosen one.

On the contrary, by making her fertile, God brands her a sinner in the eyes of all men; a sinner who has committed a crime against nature by wanting to be the equal of a man. It could also be argued that, out of a sense of guilt and masochism, Judith would be unable to accept such a fulfilment, or, in an even more profound sense, she cannot accept being a woman like any other. In front of Holofernes, who mocks her by saying 'to protect myself from you I need only to give you a child' (Act V, p. 308), she boasts that she is different from other women. A substitute penis is not enough for her: she would like to be Holofernes himself, to equal him in heroic deeds. But her desire meets only with derision: After her 'heroic deed', everyone can regard her as a hero who outshines all others, except Judith herself. She knows that she has only 'sacrificed' herself to take revenge for having been treated like a whore, for being degraded, defiled, humiliated. After the sexual act, the act of murder, any patriotic motives are forgotten. This is why she refuses to accept any reward for her action, just as she refuses (unlike the biblical Judith) to 'surrender' Holofernes' head. 'The head', phallic substitute, 'is my possession', she says (Act V, p. 315). When she decapitates Holofernes, she also reveals the meaning behind her action: 'Ha, holofernes, do you respect me now?'

Thus, by killing Holofernes, Judith takes her revenge for being nothing more than a woman, a narcissistic wound which is reopened by the first act of coitus. If Holofernes had spared her, she would never have been able to decapitate him because, unlike the biblical Judith, she cannot identify with her people – they are an only too vivid reminder of her own weakness. The Hebrews are contemptible, effeminate; her name, Judith, in so far as it symbolizes her Judaism, hurts her (cf. Act V, p. 314). She is pleased to see the Hebrews powerless, since it means she can more easily act as their substitute. In the play, the character of Ephraim symbolizes the weakness of the male sex: 'if your cowardice is that of your whole sex, if all men see in danger nothing but a warning to escape it – then a woman has won the right to do a great deed' (Act II, p. 273). By using Holofernes' own sword to decapitate him, Judith both castrates the man and takes his phallus for herself: at the same time she punishes herself, since she deprives herself of 'the first and last man on earth' (Act V, p. 319).

Judith's demand for the phallus is stressed by Mirza: 'A woman should bear men; she should never kill men!' (Act V, p. 309). As for Judith, she hides from herself the 'unnaturalness' of her action. Here the supernatural serves as a cover: only God can make a woman more courageous than a man, just as God alone can make a brother kill his brother and a mother devour her child. The episode of the prophet Daniel is necessary in order for Judith to believe even further in her own rationalizations, to convince her that the ways of God pass through sin. In reality, Judith is truly the equal of Holofernes, that other monster before whom Nature itself trembles: 'Nature trembles at the giant birth of her own womb and will not create a second man, or only that he may destroy the first' (Act II, p. 273). This 'second man' is Judith, female double of Holofernes; both are tragic heroes by virtue of their excessiveness, their ὕβρις, which places them outside the rest of humanity. Holofernes corresponds to Judith's ego-ideal: 'Oh if only I were you! Only for a day, for an hour!' (Act IV, p. 297), she says to him.

For Judith, Holofernes is both the substitute for her first love-object, her father (or God), and the man best suited to answer the demands of her wounded narcissism. Here, the choice of an object according to the anaclitic (attachment) type coincides with object-choice of a narcissistic type.[34] Holofernes himself thinks he is a God and Achior describes him to Judith using the same terms in which he described the Hebrew God to Holofernes. Holofernes is therefore truly the man who, for Judith, can replace her dead father and make her forget God. But, above all, he is the only man she would want to resemble, the only one who can both fulfil her and humiliate her: 'Every woman has a right to demand of every man that he be a hero. When you see one, does it not seem that you are seeing what you would, what you should be? A man may forgive cowardice in another; a woman never. Can you forgive a prop for breaking? You can scarcely forgive your need for a prop' (Act III, p. 276).

If Judith in Hebbel's *Judith* 'depicts' or 'stages' the taboo of virginity, then the character of Holofernes (whom Freud does not mention)[35] is no less vital to its understanding. Besides, the title of the play is *Judith and Holofernes*, and Hebbel introduces a notable balance into the play by the importance he accords respectively to the two protagonists. The first act is devoted entirely to Holofernes, the second focuses on Judith, and the third prepares the way for their meeting, which does not occur until the fourth. The destiny of Holofernes, who at first sight is so different from Manasses, is also ruled by the fear of castration. But in Holofernes' case he covers up and overcompensates for this fear by an excessive narcissism. Holofernes would like to be as omnipotent as the Hebrew God, to force the universe to its knees before him. Judith, like Achior, seems overwhelmed by such a man: 'Man, monster, you force yourself between me and my God! I must pray at this moment and cannot' (Act V, p. 307).

Nevertheless, Holofernes could never be as strong as the God of the Jews because he belongs to the world of mortals: he may have 'a countenance that is one single eye, an imperious eye, and . . . a foot from which the world he treads upon seems to shrink. But there was a time when he was not; therefore one can come when he will be no more' (Act II, p. 273). The threat of death weighs on him constantly and continually breaches his narcissism. It is in order to defend himself from the fear of death that Holofernes erects a system of megalomaniacal defences: he dreams of being able to have engendered himself, as of being able to decide the hour of his own death. Primary narcissism, in which one desires to be one's own progenitor and to be immortal, dictates Holofernes' behaviour.

But the desire to be *causa sui* also implies a corresponding desire to murder one's own parents. No allusions are made to Holofernes' father in the play. However, Nabuchodonosor can be regarded as a paternal substitute. Holofernes, in a radical departure from the biblical version, only carries out his king's orders and extends his empire so as to be more certain of one day overthrowing him. The only feeling he has for Nabuchodonosor is scorn: he makes a mockery of his 'father'. 'He takes his shining helmet in his hand and pays devotion to his own image. He has nothing to guard against except colic, in order not to make grimaces and frighten himself' (Act I, p. 261).

Ridiculed by his son, such a father could not possibly be deified. Which explains Holofernes' scepticism with regard to the deities he takes to be interchangeable, the mere products of human dictates and conventions. The only effective guarantee of divinity is force, and, it is indeed thanks to his son's force that the father, Nabuchodonosor, is regarded as a God: 'The herald will declare him God, and I am to prove to the world that he is' (Act I, p. 262). 'Mankind has one great purpose, to bring forth a god. And this god, how will he show he is a god, if he does not set himself up in eternal strife against them' (ibid.). If he is invincible, then the god of the Jews is truly a god. Unwittingly, Holofernes takes the Hebrew god as his model. But he is a parody of this God: like him, Holofernes would like to be able to 'sound the hearts and minds' of his entourage, and yet to remain himself forever a mystery to all. Just as yesterday's idol is sacrificed to today's, so each of the successive figures he assumes in order to make his escape from others more successfully becomes, in turn, fodder for a new creation. Through this endless self-creation, which is not subject to any ego-ideal, Holofernes retakes control of his own existence indefinitely, negating the primal scene and repeating the murder of the father.

By refusing to identify with a whole object, Holofernes can only deny the identity of the subject and allow each of his desires to triumph successively, in an expenditure without reserve. In this manner he feels superior to the natural elements which are all subdued by man. Perpetual self-creation also means perpetual self-murder, and thus it means believing that one can emerge from non-existence and throw oneself into it at will: 'I hack the Holofernes of today merrily into pieces and give him to the Holofernes of tomorrow to eat.'

Through these repeated creations and 'un-creations', Holofernes only desires to be at one with the eternal, self-renewing flux of life. Against the schizoid fragmentation of his ego, his only weapon is narcissistic unification and megalomaniacal defence. But in this way he condemns himself to the solitude of a god, obliged never to love anyone but himself, in the nostalgic hope of finally meeting an equal who can recognize him. He finds such an equal in Judith, but at the price of death.

Only a woman, and one who does not immediately give herself, could reassure him of his power, just as only another woman is a constant reminder of his weakness: his mother. Like all other heroes, Holofernes invents a family romance in which he attributes a fantastic origin to himself:

he was reared by a lioness and never knew his mother. For her he feels only hatred since she has given him the gift of life and, by the same token, death. To have a mother is to admit that one cannot conquer by oneself either life or death. The mother breaches all megalomaniacal defences:

> All the women of the world I am glad to see except one, and her I have never seen and will never see – my mother. I have as small a wish to see her as to see my grave. The thing that pleases me best is that I do not know where I came from . . . But what is a mother for her son? The mirror of his weakness of yesterday or tomorrow. He cannot look upon her without thinking of the time when he was a pitiful brat that paid for the few drops of milk he swallowed with smacking kisses. And if he forgets this, he sees in her a spectre that juggles age and death before him and makes his own self, his flesh and blood, repugnant to him. (Act IV, pp. 294–5)

The first narcissistic injury is inflicted by birth, which creates an orifice through which all subsequent thefts become possible. By subsequently turning her son into her own phallus, by demanding love in exchange for food, the mother robs him of part of his body, castrates him, devours him. Like Judith, Holofernes defends himself constantly against the theft of his bodily integrity: 'Then [when I was younger] I thought I was stealing my life if I did not conquer it anew every day. What was given to me as a gift, I did not think I possessed' (Act V, p. 300). To be enigmatic, to close oneself to all others, is a way also of being impenetrable, of preventing others from coming to steal one' thoughts: 'Here they skulk around me and peep into the cracks and crevices of my soul and out of every word from my mouth seek to forge a picklock for the inner chamber of my heart' (Act I, p. 259). Conversely, to eavesdrop oneself on the words of others is to admit that one's own thoughts are not omnipotent. To steal is a sign of dependency and slavery.[36] But, if Holofernes is haunted by the fear of being robbed, if he considers his mother to be 'the great thief', it is perhaps because he projects onto everyone, and particularly onto his mother, his own oral sadism. It is not by chance that there are numerous oral metaphors present in the text. Holofernes' relations with everyone, with life, with his comrades-in-arms, with women, are those of ravenous and rapacious consumption. He introjects[37] into himself the whole world, in order to assimilate it and enlarge his own ego: 'What a man sees, he becomes! The great rich world did not enter the bit of distended skin in which we live; we received eyes, so that we might gulp it down piece by piece' (Act IV, p. 295).

Death is, for him, a return to the maternal breast, to be greedily devoured once more. For Holofernes, living and dying mean sucking. Because of the fear of death 'we hold it [life] fast, and squeeze it and suck it, until it bursts into pieces.'

> Now we seek by eating to protect ourselves from being eaten and strive with our death against the teeth of the world. Which is why it is so incomparably sweet to die of life itself, to let the stream swell so that the vein which contains it bursts, to mingle the supreme bliss and the shudder of extinction ... So I would like to say some time to myself: 'Now I will die'. And if, as soon as the word is spoken, I do not vanish and am sucked up by all the thirsty lips of creation ... ? (Act IV, p. 293)

A belief in the omnipotence of thoughts which links Holofernes' narcissism to that of children and animists. But when an adult remains at the stage of infantile narcissism it is because his or her ego-ideal has not developed. Whether perverse or psychotic, Holofernes' behaviour can best be explained by Kleinian categories rather than Freudian ones. This perhaps explains why Freud remains silent about him.

Judith and Holofernes is thus a 'powerful depiction' of the taboo of virginity which allows the spectator, thanks to a supplement of fiction and illusion, to reconcile himself provisionally with his castration fantasies: a reconciliation that the analytic cure is not always certain of acheiving.[38] But to move from a dramatic to a metapsychological framework is to abandon the scenography in favour of the scenario. It is, by calling upon the literary text to testify for psychoanalysis, to inscribe it in the 'process' of truth, by 'robbing' the text of something ungraspable: a pretention, once again, to mastery and appropriation. Without remainder.

Moreover, if literature, after a reductive treatment, can seem to bend itself to an analytic reading, is it not because Freud's conceptions about women coincide with those of the literature that he exploits? An adequation between the literary and the analytic which, far from being an index of truth, is merely an index that both are in the grip of the same cultural and ideological tradition: an identity of prejudices whose constraining force imposes itself like that of truth.

Summarize, Interpret (*Gradiva*)

I must either cut nothing out, that is, refrain from making any selections, or be unfaithful to them ... and venture to make some selection or cut. But in this second hypothesis, at the first hint of unfaithfulness, at the first symptom, I am no longer myself according to them. At the first symptom, it's all an artistic technique, an artistic method, and immediately I am lost. You cannot resolve this dilemma for me: I am either stupid or unfaithful. I either attempt to exhaust every detail in all its indefiniteness, as they do, and then cannot even begin to begin. Or I relinquish the total indefiniteness of detail, even the smallest part, and then, on the other hand, I lose everything because my alleged system of security collapses.

Peguy, *Clio*[1]

Summarize, Interpret (*Gradiva*)

A dangerous short cut

Freud devotes the first part of his study of *Gradiva*[2] to summarizing the story for those readers who no longer have any clear recollection of it: this summary is intended to be brief, Freud's aim being simply 'to investigate two or three dreams to be found here and there in *Gradiva* with the help of certain analytic methods' (p. 44). It is once the summary is completed that the work of interpretation is to begin: the moment of the summary is that of a 'naive' reading of the text when the reader, swept along by the same feelings and hopes as the hero, is in too great a state of suspense to be able to understand it: 'Now that we have finished telling the story and satisfied our own suspense, we can get a better view of it, and we shall now reproduce it with the technical terminology of our science, and in doing so we shall not feel disconcerted at the necessity for repeating what we have said before' (p. 44).

Freud, from the very beginning, presents his summary as an imperfect substitute for the text itself: to summarize is necessarily to strip the text of its charms by changing the form of the narrative: it is to deprive the reader of any pleasure incentive.

> And now I ought properly to ask all my readers to put aside this little essay and instead spend some time acquainting

> themselves with *Gradiva* (which first appeared in the bookshops in 1903), so that what I refer to in the following pages will be familiar to them. But for the benefit of those who have already read *Gradiva*, I will recall the substance of the story in a brief summary; and I shall count upon their memory to restore to it all the charm of which this treatment will deprive it. (p. 10)

At the very least, the essential part of the text, its content, will remain intact. The summary will tell the same story as Jensen's text, only more succinctly and in a different, less beautiful, less poetic language.

In fact such a separation of the form and content of a text could seem suspect and throw discredit upon the Freudian undertaking. It can also seem paradoxical, given Freud's own numerous and repeated warnings against making any such division between a text's form and its content, be it the text of a dream, a delusion, or a work of art. Does not the originality of his method lie precisely in the importance he attaches to the most insignificant details? Is it not his premiss that there is nothing in the text that does not serve some purpose, nothing that is purely decorative? 'Our author, who, as we have long since realized, never introduces a single idle or unintentional feature into his text' (p. 68). 'By which end are we to take hold of a dream like this so as to fit it into the whole context, if it is not to remain no more than an unnecessary decoration of the story?' (p. 56). The paradox is even more striking given that the hero is suffering from an hysterical psychosis. Freud considers the very form of the language he uses, its ambiguity, to be an index of the double determination of his symptoms. The form of the illness itself, stemming from a conflict between two psychic agencies, dictates the form of the hero's discourse. It is because the form of Norbert's discourse seems to Freud the most symptomatic of all his symptoms that he uses it in the final part of his study as proof of the validity of his interpretation.

The Freudian method, therefore, seems necessarily to exclude any summary, any transformation of the text. Interpreting the text correctly should mean looking at the whole text, and, indeed, Freud does refer the reader first of all to the text. Nevertheless, he summarizes it; he even summarizes the dreams which are of particular interest to him: 'It is easy to give the content of this dream in brief' (p. 56). Yet Jensen himself, as if wishing to oppose in advance any cutting of the text, stresses the extremely clear and detailed nature of Norbert's dreams: 'yet the dream picture still stood most distinctly in every detail before his open eyes' (p. 22 of Jensen). The economy made on details seems even less justified when, on comparing the full dream text to Freud's summary of it (for example p. 22 of Jensen and pp. 12 and 13 of Freud), we see that what the summary omits could, reinserted into the general context of the story, have thrown valuable light on the dreamer's behaviour and furthered the work of interpretation. Thus the detailed description of the eruption of Vesuvius and the terror it inspires in Norbert allows us to add a further, punitive sense to the dream's erotic meaning. The masses of flame from the crater, the ashes that rain down are all so many 'details' Freud neglects, yet they recur on numerous occasions in the story. Could this simply be a case of 'idle repetition'?[3]

Why does Freud break the rules of his own method?[4] Why are some details overshadowed in favour of others which are foregrounded? What principle of selection is in operation here, what determines what the summary includes or omits? In summarizing a text, is one only suppressing its 'charm'? Or is it equally a case of transforming its content, producing what is already a different text? If, in order to make a correct study of the text, one must look at it in its totality, then the summary seems like a useless supplement tacked onto a text that is already full of meaning. Useless and even dangerous, since while giving the impression of faithfully reproducing the text's content and merely removing the pleasure incentive, it would in fact be suppressing part of its sense. This 'dangerous supplement', is it really superfluous, or does it have a precise function within the Freudian method?

At the beginning of the second section, after he has made his 'summary', Freud feigns astonishment at having been led to do something completely different from his stated intentions: far from providing a brief summary, what he has in fact done is to launch into a veritable dismemberment of the text.

> How has it come about ... that we have been led into dissecting the whole story and examining the mental processes in the two chief characters? This has not in fact been an unnecessary piece of work; it was an essential preliminary ... It is even my view that we are still not free to turn to our proper task but that we must linger a little more over the story itself and carry out some further preliminary work. (p. 41)

If, intending to analyse a few dreams, Freud breaks up the whole structure of the text, he does not do so unwittingly, and as if motivated by an unconscious desire. The dissection is not 'an unnecessary piece of work'. It finds its methodological justification in the impossibility of analysing dreams out of context, in isolation from the particular code of this or that dreamer. The time of the interpretation is always retrospective: very often a dream can only be understood with the aid of another dream, itself produced by one or other of the day's events. 'A short dream which he had in his albergo in Rome ... throws a retrospective light on the erotic drift of his first major dream' (p. 67). A summary of the work is necessary to provide the dream's context: its context is decisive in determining its code. The selection operated by the summary is a function of this finality. Henceforth the summary no longer appears to be a useless supplement but a complement to the method of interpretation. It is designed to prepare the way for interpretation since, as a whole, Jensen's text, by the excess of meaning it conveys, conceals the fact that of itself it is not fully transparent. The summary is not a supplement added to the text, a surplus: it comes to reveal the gaps hidden in the text's continuity and plenitude. The dismemberment of the text introduces ruptures, discontinuities and cuts into its seamless fabric. In order to construct, the analytic work always begins by *de*constructing. It is the summary that performs this deconstructive function.

If the summary is a complement to the text, what does it add to it? Despite the dissection Freud admits he has carried out, he claims at the end of the first section to have stuck to the text and to have made no additions to it. No supplementary interpretation has been slipped into the summary. Despite the cuts and displacements it effects, the summary remains faithful to the story: it is the author himself who has provided the text and the commentary:

> But how if, on being questioned, he [the author] were completely to deny any such purpose? It is so easy to draw analogies and to read meanings into things. Is it not rather we who have slipped into this charming poetic story a secret meaning very far from its author's intentions? Possibly. We shall have to come back to this question later. For the moment, however, we have tried to save ourselves from making any such tendentious interpretation by giving the story almost entirely in the author's own words. Anyone who compares our reproduction with the actual text of *Gradiva* will have to concede us that much. (p. 43)

> But I should not in fact have ventured to present this piece of interpretative work to my readers, if the author had not at this point lent me his powerful assistance. (p. 82)

> As always happens at specially difficult points, the author once more comes to our help here. (p. 83)

On several occasions, even when he appears to have abandoned the preliminary work to begin what is, properly speaking, the work of analysis, Freud repeats his assertion that he has used nothing but the text itself (pp. 82, 83, 88). The key to its decipherment lies within the text itself and, to some extent, the three sections which follow the summary merely repeat what it says. Freud postpones the moment when he will finally have to leave the text behind. At the beginning of the third section he writes:

> In the further course of the story there is yet another dream which may perhaps tempt us even more than the first to try to translate it and insert it into the train of events in the hero's mind. But we should save very little by diverging from the author's account and hurrying on immediately to this second dream; for no one who wishes to analyse someone else's dream can avoid turning his attention in the greatest detail to all the dreamer's experiences, both external and internal. It will probably be best, therefore, to keep close to the thread of the story and to intersperse it with our glosses as we proceed. (p. 64)

Interpretation is thus reduced to glosses: this is the only supplement.

> *Gloss*: annotation between the lines or in the margin of a text to explain a difficult word, elucidate an obscure passage. By extension , commentary, explanatory note.
>
> *Commentary*: collection of explanations, remarks made of/on a text. See paraphrase. More or less superfluous addition to a story. (*Petit Robert*)[5]

The Freudian gloss seems to imply the double meaning of the term: to be both an unnecessary supplement, more impoverished than the text which it, as it were, merely paraphrases; and at the same time to be an indispensable complement: the gloss makes the text become what it is by transforming obscurity into clarity and making what is implicit explicit. Understood in this double sense, the gloss would allow one both to be faithful to the text *and* to explain it. But which text are we talking about? Jensen's – as summarized by Freud. The interpretation – gloss is made on a mutilated, dissected text, one already subjected to the necessary work, the necessary torture to make its meaning apparent. The text – summary is a text already selected by the future interpretation: thus it is hardly surprising that this interpretation can make it intelligible. The text–summary must be seen as a theoretical object, a laboratory product manufactured by science.

The product of a method, this method can then be applied to it. Freud's summary is not there to refresh the reader's memory. It does not exist prior to the interpretation; the summary is the product of the interpretation at the same time as determining it. It is the laboratory preparation of Jensen's text: without it, the text would remain inaccessible to science. In this sense it is necessary.

Transformations

If we take Freud's invitation to compare his account to that of Jensen literally, we are struck by a whole series of transformations. The effect of these changes is to deprive the work of its charm. This effect is intended to show not that the 'form' of the narrative is superfluous and dissociable from its content, but to show that it has a very specific function: to seduce the reader with a pleasure incentive that keeps him or her in a state of illusion and distracts him or her from the 'real' meaning of the text. The pleasure incentive that a naive reading of the text offers the reader is part of the implicit contract between author and reader.

The reader agrees for the duration of the text to enter into a delusion, to identify and sympathize with the hero and heroine, to believe in spectres and phantoms, in return for a little aesthetic pleasure and a further, deeper yield of pleasure: that derived from the release of repressed impulses.[6] In *Gradiva* Jensen does not respect the contract: the reader, believing himself to be normal, the standard of humanity, can no longer identify with the protagonist once he realizes that, in fact, he is dealing with someone suffering from delusions. He has been duped by the author: the hero's madness is too private and peculiar for it to coincide with the reader's own fantasies and arouse his interest.[7] By voluntarily stripping the text of its charm, Freud denounces the unacknowledged mercantile relationship between author and reader, and the opposition between the normal and the pathological on which it rests.

So long as the reader remains under the spell of the text and its 'hero', he is as deluded as Norbert, who lets himself fall under the spell of a classical statue. Freud's aim is to show that every reader daily transgresses the fictional and conventional boundaries separating the normal from the pathological.[8] To refuse to identify with Norbert is to refuse to acknowledge there is only a difference of degree between so-called 'normal' passion and delusion. The lover too is possessed and fascinated by his object and, like Norbert, in search of a lost object, one loved during childhood. Norbert's obsession with the stone image is no more than a magnifying paradigm of all love.[9]

To change the text is to force the reader to renounce his illusion and the enjoyment of his fantasies. It forces him to confront his own lack of superiority: textual transformation has a purgative function. However, if it deprives the reader's ego of its bonus of seduction, it does offer him some compensation. If instead he turns his attention to the search for the real meaning of the text, he will experience the 'intellectual' pleasure of solving a mystery.[10] The mystery of the delusion, of the literary text whose 'form' is a facade, a veil that must be unravelled thread by thread. To summarize the text is to work simultaneously towards the erosion of three delusions – those of hero, author and reader. It is to shatter the complicity of a seamless text which by its very coherence conceals the fact that it is enigmatic. To dissect the text is to bring to light its lacunae, the absence of links between certain events or the substitution of fictitious links for those which really exist. Deconstruction of the text is an essential first step in the reconstruction of another, different text, by weaving different connections between events and introducing a new necessity. To summarize is to isolate the different elements from the narrative web in which they are caught and to weave them together to form a different pattern:[11] 'On the day after their second meeting in the house of Meleager, he had all kinds of strange and apparently unconnected experiences' (p. 72).

What Freud does in his analysis of the supposedly absurd dream can be used as a paradigm for understanding his process of dissecting Jensen's text as a whole. First of all he breaks up the manifest text of the dream and examines each fragment separately. He then reconstructs another text (the latent content) by using his own associations in the place of Norbert's. It is because the latter is unaware of the real links between the day's different events, and has replaced them with secondary rationalizations which he only half believes, that he has an obscure dream in which all the day's different elements are jumbled.

> Are we to venture on an attempt at interpreting this dream too – that is at replacing it by the latent thoughts from whose distortions it must have arisen? It is as senseless as only a dream can be expected to be; and this absurdity of dreams is the mainstay of the view which refuses to characterise dreams as completely valid acts and maintains they arise out of a purposeless excitation of the elements of the mind. We are able to apply to this dream the technique which may be described as the regular procedure for interpreting dreams. It consists in paying no attention to the apparent connections in the manifest dream, but in fixing our eyes upon each portion of its content independently, and in looking for its origin in the dreamer's impressions, memories and free associations. Since, however, we cannot question Hanold, we shall have to content ourselves with referring to his impressions and we may very tentatively put our own associations in place of his. (p. 73)

Nevertheless, Freud does not examine, fragment by fragment, the whole text. The summary not only fragments, it also selects. Freud's attention is more directed than free-floating. Even when certain passages are quoted in their entirety, they are not faithful and strict repetitions of the initial text: inserted into another context the quotations set Jensen's text in movement,[12] unsettle it, take it to a different place. The end result of the selection of material in the summary is that certain elements are brought together or isolated. A series of displacements is effected which are always highly revealing. Freud's cuts allow him to associate what in the hero's conscious remains as yet unconnected. The reader's understanding is thus more advanced than the hero's. The cuts pave the way for the solution of the mystery and the hero's cure.

The aim of the summary is to make the text intelligible by ignoring what is considered to be superfluous. Descriptions of Pompeii, the surrounding countryside and the climate are all either abridged or ignored by Freud, deemed to have an illusive or seductive function. Explanations of the hero's behaviour internal to the work itself (either Jensen's or Norbert's) are accorded the status of secondary rationalizations and are, to a greater or lesser extent, dismissed: they would only serve as impediments to any genuine investigation.

In fact, what is treated as a facade, what the summary sets out to explode, could perhaps serve another function within the narrative: to reply to a need that is both psychological and structural. Psychological, because the spacing of events indicates the distance that separates the hero from a full understanding of his behaviour, a distance filled not only with a series of rationalizations but also with events that could lead to the resolution of his delusion. Structural, because, in order for the narrative to be able to continue, it is necessary for Norbert not to understand what is happening and for the reader to remain uncertain what literary genre he is dealing with.

The demands of the narrative are, in fact, directly opposed to those of the summary. The former requires the maximum prolongation of the mystery and the postponement of the story's end. To omit a detailed account of all

Norbert's fantasies is, in itself, to transform him: he become less sick than he is. Just as the summary necessarily shortens the narrative, it also accelerates the cure.

For example, Norbert only gradually comes to understand the symbolic link formed by his unconscious between the honeymooning couples and the houseflies. What he does notice almost immediately is that both annoy him intensely. In the summary, Freud immediately connects the two, lovers and flies, by using the metaphor of the swarm to designate the stream of couples heading to Italy on their honeymoon. This metaphor serves a didactic function comparable to the analyst's invention of the verbal bridge to enable his patient to associate more easily, to move from conscious to unconscious meaning:[13] 'He found himself among a swarm of honeymooners' (p. 15).

A few lines further on, he introduces a technical term justifying the invention of the metaphor: 'The part which has so far been played by the honeymooning couples, who had troubled his spirits and harassed his thoughts, was now taken over by the horseflies . . . The two sorts of tormenting spirits melted into a unity' (pp. 15–16).[14] The principle which guides the selection and determines what will be cut from the summary is the future interpretation, which retains only what is essential to its purposes. Jensen's description of Gradiva is a portrait in classical rhetorical style. Freud retains only one specific element from it: the vertical position of Gradiva's foot; a significant and exceptional detail[15] which, by virtue of the affect it produces in Norbert, is that trace which opens the readable space of the text,[16] a trace which, taken literally, determines the hero's departure for Pompeii in search of its imprint; the trace of the lost object, covered over by the literalness of the language.

The summary keeps quiet about a number of elements which, in fact, play a decisive role in what follows: in the very beginning, when Norbert, contemplating the statue, begins to fantasize, he imagines a golden and green lizard disappearing between the paving stones at the approach of the young Pompeian girl (cf. pp. 16–17 of Jensen). This lizard is mentioned only towards the end of the summary, in connection with the absurd dream. Freud omits any mention of the fact that it was on his return from a previous visit to Pompeii that Norbert had become convinced Gradiva must have lived there. Not only does this information make the delusional construction seem more realistic, but it also immediately links his decision to make a second journey to the flight from erotic desires in obedience to the superego. Everything takes place as if Freud wanted to delete a certain number of clues present in the text, so as to make the story seem even more bizarre and mysterious and to justify a necessary recourse to the analytic method. Thus he 'forgets' that Jensen explains why Norbert has repressed his erotic life: from childhood he has been destined to follow the family tradition, to follow in his father's footsteps (cf. pp. 25 and 45 of Jensen and p. 14 of Freud).

Another characteristic piece of forgetfulness: the verses from Ovid that Norbert remembers: 'her floating vest/a polished buckle clasped./Her careless locks/in simple knot were gathered' (p. 52 of Jensen). By erasing these verses, Freud suppresses the 'minimal resemblance' around which the delusion concerning the clasp attached 'to the sun' is woven.

The effect of the selection is either to make what is not (or does not seem to be) mysterious into a mystery, or to erase what is truly puzzling. The summary not only fragments, and selects from, the text, it also puts into operation a whole series of semantic substitutions. It is the translation from one language into another. These transformations move in the direction of a certain interpretation of the characters' behaviour. They turn a singular and concrete adventure into a more general and abstract tale. Even the character's emotional states are transposed into a more general and abstract key. For example, Jensen writes:

> To this she was equally silent, only about her lips there was a silent quiver as if she were repressing a burst of laughter. Now a feeling of fright came upon him; apparently she was

> sitting there before him like a silent image, a phantom to whom speech was denied. Consternation at this discovery was stamped fully and distinctly upon his features. (p. 56)

Transcribed into the summary, Norbert's terror becomes a feeling of the vaguest kind: 'On the basis of his latest theories of her origin he addressed her in Greek and waited with trepidation to learn whether, in her phantom presence, she possessed the power of speech' (p. 18 of Freud). Is not the precise quality of the affect produced vitally important? And does not this passage from the singular to the universal, the concrete to the abstract, indicate resistance to a certain interpretation?

In more general terms, the transformation of the text involves replacing descriptions and metaphors by concepts designed to make them intelligible: the summary is already an explanation. This passage towards the concept is a movement towards reason, towards univocity of meaning. By calling things by their proper names, Freud prevents the reader from falling into a delusion, from falling asleep, from dreaming, from falling under the spell of the text's poetry. Thus Zoe, in calling Norbert by his name, brings his delusion to an end: 'As everyone knows, the best method of waking a sleeper or a sleep-walker is to call him by his own name' (p. 27 of Jensen). The slide from one language into another effects an economy of signs (the summary abridges) and a movement from poetry, which contains the truth without being aware of it, to science, which delivers this truth up in proper and adequate terms. The substitution, if carried through to completion, would put an end to the story by revealing the truth.

For example, whereas Jensen wants to leave the reader in doubt, describing the hero's behaviour as oscillating between conscious and unconscious, between dream and waking reality, Freud very quickly introduces the clinical concept of a *delusion*: the key to the mystery. (cf. pp. 50 and 51 of Jensen and p. 18 of Freud). Other examples are: Freud twice uses the technical term identification (pp. 16 and 33); he substitutes the concept of fantasy for the description of specific fantasies, which means the translator is spared the effort of looking closely at the hero's imaginative output. Thus Freud (on p. 11) summarizes the latter by writing 'little by little he brought the whole of his archaeological learning into the service of these and other fantasies relating to the original who had been the model for the relief'. These fantasies take up several pages in the story: 'as he contemplated the girl, her immediate and more remote environment rose before his imagination like an actuality. It created for him, with the aid of his knowledge of antiquity, the vista of a long street, among the houses of which were temples and porticos etc., etc.' (p. 16 of Jensen).

The summary's explanatory aims are revealed by a certain number of 'digressions' designed to supplement the absence of authorial explanations and throw light on the hero's behaviour. Thus the first break in the narration of the story is motivated by Norbert's incomprehensible character: 'Let us pause for a moment at this journey, planned for such remarkable incogent reasons, and take a closer look at our hero's personality and behaviour. He still appears to us as incomprehensible and foolish' (p. 14 of Freud). When Zoe leaves her sketchbook behind, Freud, without introducing the actual term, takes the opportunity to explain that her action is a parapraxis: 'We should be inclined to regard her having forgotten the book as a pledge of her return, for it is our belief that no-one forgets anything without some secret reason or hidden motive' (p. 22). There follows a lengthy digression on the subject of repression and its mechanisms, in which Jensen's descriptions, certain pictorial representations (in particular one by Felicien Rops) and a pathological case from Freud's own clinical experience are all cited as proof of his hypothesis.

In a later passage, Norbert's desire to touch Gradiva's hand is imputed to an act of sexual aggression, a man's duty in lovemaking (p. 38). When Freud does not himself offer an aid to interpretation, it is because he finds one in the text, and he congratulates the novelist or Zoe on their perspicacity (cf. pp. 21 and 22, 38 and 39). Finally, he adds a few remarks on Norbert's critical mind (pp. 20, 23, 25) and on Zoe's emotional state, which would explain her behaviour (p. 21), etc.

As a consequence of the summary's didactic aims, certain parts of the text are displaced and juxtaposed with others to make them intelligible. Thus to explain that Norbert, until the time he is obliged to study women's and girls' feet, has never paid the slightest attention to the female sex, Freud adds that 'social duties had always seemed to him an unavoidable nuisance' (p. 12). A remark which is indeed present almost word for word in Jensen's story, but in a completely different context (p. 26 of Jensen).

Thus the summary, which prepares for the work of analysis, explodes the initial text. A completely different textual play is offered to the reader who has not taken the trouble to consult Jensen's text. The latter remains only in a 'truncated and distorted form, like a mutilated telegraph message'.[17] The summary is deadly, not by virtue of its brevity, but because it effects a transposition from one language to another: to a much more univocal language which forces the text out of its undecidability.[18]

The symbolism of Pompeii

Has Freud really left it to the author to provide both text and commentary? Does not the summary have the effect of privileging the analytic interpretation over all others? Does it not erase the plurality of codes in the text to the benefit of one code alone?

For example, there can be no doubt that, if we confine ourselves to the summary, it seems certain that Pompeii symbolizes repression. By inventing this symbolism, by deliberately using Zoe as its mouthpiece and by showing how Norbert makes a travesty of it in his delusion, the dupe of this same symbolism, Jensen is showing that he has an endopsychic knowledge of repression: he is describing the process of repression in symbolic terms, completely accurately yet unaware he is doing so.

> There is, in fact, no better analogy for repression, by which something in the mind is at once made inaccessible and preserved, than burial of the sort to which Pompeii fell a victim and from which it could emerge once more only through the work of spades. Thus it was that the young archaeologist was obliged in his phantasy to transport to Pompeii the original of the relief which reminded him of the object of his youthful love.[19] (p. 40)

Admittedly, it is Jensen's text that permits such an interpretation. The author goes as far as to suggest a contrast between Norbert's science, the knowledge of dead languages and archaeology which enables him to decipher in expert fashion the mysteries of Pompeii,[20] and his ignorance of his own internal Pompeii. Here science is no longer of any use to him, and he needs Zoe to rescue him from living death. Is this not to emphasize his kinship to Oedipus?

But the text, taken as a whole, offers other codes for its decipherment. One signifier in particular is privileged over all others: the sun. In the *Postscript to the Second Edition*, Freud remarks that the central situation of *Gradiva* is the same in all Jensen's novels: 'the apparition in the midday glare of a summer's day of a girl who has died (or was believed to have died)' (p. 94). The importance of the sun is contrasted, rhetorically, to rain, darkness and ash. The Italian spring or summer sunshine contrasted to the wintry cold of north Germany. The sun, source of the delusion (which reaches its crisis when the sun is at its strongest) but also source of the cure: the canary sings when the sun shines. Norbert's first meeting with Zoe's father takes place in bright sunshine. 'The Sun' is the name of the inn where, unknown to Norbert who usually stays at The Diomed, Zoe and her father (a possible obstacle) are staying. The flowers of love, the rose and poppy, are associated with the sun, as is the Vesuvio wine whose grapes ripen in its glare and which, with the sun, contributes to Norbert's feelings of dizziness and confusion, making him feel not at all his usual self:

> It seemed to him that the dark shadows of the tree-tops and the buildings did not stay in the same place. Of course on the ground of this region – unsteady from ancient times – this could not be exactly surprising, for the subterranean glow lurked everywhere, after an eruption, and let a little of itself rise in the vines and grapes from which was pressed Vesuvio, which was not one of Norbert Hanold's usual evening drinks. (pp. 60–1 of Jensen)

In the sun the lizard basks and the flies are at their most annoying. Zoe's whole personality – her Christian name signifying 'life' and her surname, Bertgang, 'the one splendid in walking' – is solar. She makes her first appearance to Norbert at noon, the hour when ghosts return from the dead. She is linked to the cult of the sun, her clothes are yellow, her sandals gold. There is always a sparkle in her eyes. She asks Norbert if he did not find his brooch in the sun. Finally, the story ends with her crossing to the other side of the street over the paving stones, in full sunlight.

Freud simply notes that Jensen considers the sun and wine to be catalysts in Norbert's delusions, but for him these are merely rationalizations designed to disguise the real source of the delusion. He also stresses the importance of the play on the word 'sun' in Norbert's absurd dream ('Somewhere in the sun Gradiva sat', p. 78 of Jensen). But, in spite of this, he does not go into the author's privileging of the signifier 'sun'. Comparing Jensen's text to Freud's summary we find the word sun on pages 17, 18, 20, 23, 25, 26, 28, 38, 40, 52, 65, 71, 72, 78, 81, 82, 84 of Freud and pages 13, 16, 22, 23, 27, 28, 31, 35, 37, 41, 44, 45, 48, 49, 50, 51, 54, 57, 59, 61, 63, 72, 74, 78, 81, 92, 93, 99, 106, 107, 108 of Jensen.[21]

Certain elements in the text can be systematically grouped together. In the first group are: Zoe, sun, light, noon, summer, vegetation, red flowers, Italy, Vesuvio wine, love, life, living languages, the conscious. In opposition we have: Norbert, cold, clouds, rain, winter, Germany, isolation, sleep, science (to be more specific, archaeology), fathers (of the two protagonists), asphodels (flower of death), dead languages, empty silence, mineral, stone, the stone statue, pumice stone, Vesuvian lava, the unconscious.[22]

Finally, there are the neutral signifiers which facilitate the passage from one group to another and which undermine the oppositions. These are: spring (intermediary season which brings the desire to travel), the imagination, dreams (daydreams or dreams proper) – a state midway between conscious and unconscious – the delusional crisis which breaks through the hero's critical judgement, Vesuvius as a powerful source of confusion and dizziness, and finally Pompeii: undecidable town *par excellence*, both ancient and modern (p. 41 of Jensen), scorched by light and sun but also enveloped by grey fumes and submerged in ash and lava. A dead town, but at the same time a place of initiation into the mysteries of life and love, as its surviving frescos show (pp. 76, 78, 183 of Jensen). A town with a double language, that of the living, the polyglots, and that of the dead, who once spoke Latin or Greek and now maintain an empty silence (pp. 40, 45–6, 48 of Jensen). A treacherous place where the hero finds precisely that love he has been trying to flee, a town whose inhabitants, whether dead or alive, male or female, seem to be of a bizarre and mysterious nature. Pompeii, cleverly chosen as the site of the crisis and the place where all certainties founder.

However, if we take into account all the elements of the symbolism, if we do not follow Freud in collapsing the different layers of symbolism in the text because they serve only to cover up the principal signification of the story – that of repression – then *Gradiva* can be interpreted in a different way. If we do not decide that there is a single meaning, thereby putting an end to the duplicity of the town and the hero's crisis, but instead remain open to the plurality of codes in the text, then *Gradiva* can also be interpreted as a 'charming poetic story' (p. 43 of Freud) which tells of the necessity for all men, on pain of madness, to obey the laws of nature and accept their fate: to pass from winter to summer, from unconscious to conscious, from death to life.

Gradiva can be read as a variation on *King Lear*, in the light of Freud's interpretation of the latter several years later. Freud himself seems to suggest a parallel between the two texts. In effect, it is *Lear* which comes to mind when he wants to demonstrate that it is possible for a writer to begin by taking an improbable premiss and then build on it in a realistic way: which is also what Jensen has supposedly done in *Gradiva* (cf. p. 43 of Freud). The reference to *Lear* seems even less arbitrary when, in the *Postscript to the Second Edition*, we read that 'by the combination of *Gradiva* and some other fragments in Florence and Munich, two reliefs were obtained, each representing three figures, who seem to be identified as the Horae, the goddesses of vegetation, and the deities of the fertilizing dew who are allied to them'. In *The Theme of the Three Caskets*, Freud writes:

> The Horae were originally goddesses of the waters of the sky, dispensing rain and dew, and of the clouds, from which rain falls; and, since the clouds were conceived of as something that has been spun, it came about that these goddesses were looked upon as spinners, an attribute that then became attached to the Moerae. In the sun-favoured Mediterranean lands it is the rain on which the fertility of the soil depends, and thus the Horae become vegetation goddesses. The beauty of the flowers and the abundance of the fruit was their doing, and they were accredited with a wealth of agreeable and charming traits. They became the divine representatives of the seasons and it is possibly owing to this connection that there were three of them ... for the peoples of antiquity at first distinguished only three seasons ... The Horae thus became the guardians of natural law and of the divine order which causes the same things to recur in Nature in an unalterable sequence ... The nature-myth changed into a human myth: the weather goddesses became goddesses of

> fate . . . The ineluctable severity of law and its relation to death and dissolution, which had been avoided in the charming figures of the Horae, were now stamped upon the Moerae, as though men had only perceived the full seriousness of natural law when they had to submit their own selves to it.[23]

Necessity for Lear to submit to death, and for Norbert to submit to life and love which are, in fact, one and the same: everyone must pay nature its dues, no-one has the right to bury himself or herself alive. Norbert is struck by madness for having attempted to transgress the laws of nature. No longer seeing or understanding anything, speaking only dead languages, he is, before finding Zoe again, truly one of the living dead. Zoe, goddess of vegetation, worshipper of the cult of the sun, revives him. But acceptance of life is also acceptance of death when the time comes. The most beautiful of women is also death; 'The great Mother-goddesses of the oriental peoples, however, seem to have been both goddesses of life and fertility, and goddesses of death' (ibid., p. 299).

The plurality of codes

To interpret Jensen's text in this way is not to refute the Freudian interpretation nor to reject a psychoanalytic form of interpretation since, once again, it is Freud himself who has permitted and even encouraged us to do so. But such a reading takes into account the whole text, which enables us to understand better than the summary does why Norbert has buried himself alive: family tradition has clipped the wings of his desire and has kept him, like the canary, behind bars since birth. Translated into the language of analysis, Norbert is born castrated. Surprisingly, Freud neglects a whole series of signs pointing in this direction. Admittedly, at the end of the summary, when referring to the dream in which Norbert imagines himself being captured like a lizard by Zoe, Freud suggests an interpretation that highlights

Norbert's masochism. But he quickly moves on and omits any mention of the lizard's appearance in Norbert's earliest fantasies: even in these, it is at the approach of the Pompeiian girl that the lizard flees under the stones.

The text also suggests a parallel between Zoe's father, the lizard-catcher who neglects his daughter, and Norbert's own father who, even before his son is born, destines him 'to preserve, if possible to exalt by that very activity [of university professor and antiquarian], the glory of his father's name' (p. 25 of Jensen). A homosexual passivity on Norbert's part towards his father and towards Zoe, with whom he exchanged blows in childhood. The unconscious identification between flies and women suggests Norbert was much more aggressed by Zoe than he would have liked, and that he did not return the treatment. To be cured is, for him, to be able to be aggressive towards her in turn, to kill the fly resting on her hand with a blow (p. 89). To be cured is to have a fly-swat.

Flies have the same effect on him as the appearance of Gradiva: they paralyse him:

> From the common fly, however, there was no protection and it paralysed, disturbed and finally shattered the psychic life of human beings, their capacity for thinking and working, every lofty flight of imagination and every beautiful feeling ... the Etruscan 'scaccia-mosche', a wooden handle with a bunch of fine leather strips fastened to it, proved the following: they had destroyed the most exalted poetic thoughts in the mind of Aeschylus ... Norbert felt in his soul that the service of a human being was to be estimated above all according to the number of flies he had killed, pierced, burned up or exterminated in hecatombs during his life, as avenger of his whole race from remotest antiquity. For the achievement of such fame, he lacked here the necessary weapon, and like the greatest battle hero of antiquity who had, however, been alone and unable to do otherwise, he left the field or rather his room, in view of the hundredfold overwhelming number of the common foe. (p. 39 of Jensen)

When he sees Gradiva and especially when he sees her manner of walking, he is rooted to the spot (pp. 51, 65, 84). Freud omits any mention of Norbert's fantasies about the Pompeiian fruit sellers: these again seem to suggest a fear of women, of woman who seduces and ensnares: 'At the street corner sat a woman offering vegetables and fruit for sale from baskets; from a half-dozen large walnuts she had removed half the shell to show the meat, fresh and sound, as a temptation for purchasers ... There Gradiva walked over the stepping stones and scared away from them a shimmering golden-green lizard' (pp. 16–17).

Finally, while it is the case that the name the hero invents, 'Gradiva', can be read as a translation of the German name 'Bertgang', it is equally true that Gradiva is an epithet of the warrior god Mars Gradivus (p. 15 of Jensen, p. 50 of Freud). Jensen emphasizes the singularity of this association between a young girl and a male god. Gradiva would be analagous to Athena, the warrior virgin, whom men dared not approach for fear of being paralysed by the Medusa's head engraved on her breastplate.[24] Petrified[25] by Zoe in his childhood, Norbert in turn transforms her into a stone statue, as one of his dreams shows. An appalling and terrifying dream in which, once more, Norbert flees before the masses of red flame pouring from the crater and in which he sees Gradiva change into a marble statue (pp. 20–1 of Jensen). Freud himself calls the stone image 'the premiss on which all that follows depends' (p. 42 of Freud). Stone, the symbol of coldness and death, of the deafness and negative hallucination that grips Norbert,[26] but also the symbol of castration and defence against castration.[27]

Perhaps Norbert's paralysis at the sight of women should be related to his fascination with the vertical angle of Gradiva's foot. Freud draws no conclusions from this idiosyncratic positioning of the foot, despite the fact that Jensen repeatedly emphasizes it. He also neglects to mention that Norbert has to ask a friend whether a woman's way of walking is different from a man's. The reason for these omissions lies in his refusal to put a fetishistic interpretation on Norbert's behaviour: such would be the interpretation favoured by traditional psychology, which bases its study on the content of the delusion (p. 45 of Freud). If the various elements in the text to which Freud pays little or no attention are brought together, one can imagine that Norbert must have become estranged from Zoe during the phallic phase of his development. The question which causes him such anxiety during his delusional crisis can be interpreted as the question of whether Gradiva has a penis or not. The obsessional question: is Gradiva alive or not, 'Is she a living person or a ghost?', is merely a displacement of the hysterical question: 'Is she a man or a woman?'

Norbert's burning desire to know is a sublimation of the desire to see and touch the female sex, the desire to touch what cannot be seen from a distance but which, nevertheless, might exist.[28] 'But the problem of the "bodily nature" of Gradiva, which pursued him all day, cannot disavow its origin in a young man's erotic curiosity about a woman's body' (p. 79 of Freud).

What Freud does not emphasize is that the principal source of Norbert's anxiety is his fear that, if he were to try and touch the young girl's hand, he would encounter nothing, the void: 'Yet Norbert was overwhelmed with the idea that if he should touch her, even lightly place his hand on hers, he would encounter only empty air' (p. 73 of Jensen). 'With this blow there came to him, for the first time, sense, consternation and also a joyous fear. He had delivered the stroke not through empty air but on an undoubtedly real, living and warm human hand' (ibid., p. 89).

Should we reproach Freud for having read the text incorrectly, for not having known how to interpret it, for having forgotten to say everything? Do we want to add our own supplement to his interpretation? No, because Freud is well aware that the hero's behaviour can be given a masochistic interpretation, as the final remarks of his study show. But he refuses to follow this line of investigation, in order to stress, so he says, the distance between fictional and real people: 'But we must stop here or we may really forget that

Hanold and Gradiva are only creatures of their author's mind.' This seems more like a quip than a convincing explanation, given that Freud's whole study has been aimed, on the contrary, at effacing this opposition.

By refusing, at the end of his study, to pursue a new line of enquiry, yet while at the same time suggesting it, Freud intends rather to show that interpretation of either real or fictional beings is always speculative and cannot lay any claim to exhaustivity. An interpretation is a call for other interpretations. The psychoanalyst holds neither the key to the story nor the key to the truth: he is not Zoe. He can only elucidate a theoretical object, one created by his science. By suggesting that his reading is partial, in both senses of the word, Freud opens the text up to other readings, and warns against the dangers of too dogmatic and reductive an interpretation. Freud's interpretation is a rewriting of Jensen's text, a different textual play, a different story, even if it is the author who, to some extent, has provided both the text and the commentary.

Double meanings

Nevertheless, Freud does privilege the given psychoanalytic interpretation above any other. The proof of its validity? The very special use of words and speeches with double meanings in Jensen's text.

> Here then we seem to have finished off the interpretation of this second dream as well. Both of them have been made intelligible to us on the presupposition that a dreamer knows in his unconscious thoughts all that he has forgotten in his conscious ones, and that in the former he judges correctly what in the latter he misunderstands in a delusion. In the course of our arguments we have no doubt been obliged to make some assertions which have seemed strange to the reader because of their unfamiliarity; and we have probably often raised a suspicion that what we pretended was the

> author's meaning was in fact only our own. I am anxious to do all I can to dissipate this suspicion; and for that reason, I will gladly enter into more detail over one of the most delicate points – I mean the use of ambiguous words and phrases such as 'somewhere in the sun Gradiva was sitting'. Anyone who reads Gradiva must be struck by the frequency with which the author puts ambiguous remarks into the mouths of his two principal characters. (pp. 83–4 of Freud)

Ambiguous discourse predominates because of the very content of the story. Once again Jensen is offering us evidence of his perfect understanding of mental processes: the ambiguity of the language is simply an extension of the double determination of the symptoms. Ambiguous writing is symptomatic of a drama played out on a double scene. The very plasticity of the verbal material allows the double intention of the discourse to be expressed clearly. More than the actions, it is the language that reveals the double – both conscious and unconscious – origin of the symptoms: 'Thus in the very products of Hanold's delusional phantasies and actions we already find a double set of determinants, a derivation from two different sources. One of these is the one that was manifest to Hanold himself, the other is the one which is revealed to us when we examine his mental processes' (p. 51–2 of Freud). 'One might be described as lying on the surface and covering the other, which was, as it were, concealed behind it. The scientific motivation might be said to serve as a pretext for the unconscious erotic one' (p. 52 of Freud).

> But whence comes this striking preference for ambiguous speeches in *Gradiva*? It is no chance event, so it seems to us, but a necessary consequence of the premisses of the story. It is nothing other than a counterpoint to the twofold determination of symptoms, in so far as speeches are themselves symptoms and, like them, arise from compromises between the conscious and unconscious. It is simply that this double origin is more easily noticed in speeches than, for instance, in actions. (p. 85 of Freud)[29]

Jensen's genius lies in the way he condenses the language of the delusion and that of the truth into a single formula:

> Exactly as it [the word] is and as it stands in the sentence, it is able, thanks to favourable circumstances, to express two different meanings. Examples of this are at our disposal in plenty. One of Napoleon III's first acts when he assumed power was to seize on the property of the House of Orleans. This excellent play on words was current at the time: '*C'est le premier vol de l'aigle*' ['It is the eagle's first "*vol*"']. '*Vol*' means 'flight' but also 'theft'.[30]

The pleasure caused by puns,[31] as by any ambiguous discourse, stems from the saving of mental energy: condensation realizes an economy of expression. Thus, thanks to the double meaning of the word '*vol*', one is spared the effort of having to express a second thought. The latter then disappears without leaving a substitute. But the pleasure yielded by this economy is only a fore-pleasure that allows the mechanism of repression to be relaxed. Jokes and word play are attempts to express, without having to do so openly, a forbidden erotic or aggressive meaning. Tendentious word play will 'evade restrictions and open sources of pleasure that have become inaccessible'.[32] Puns avoid the necessity of having to express a second thought which is critical of the first. Words which condense several senses apart from their own proper meaning, and processes similar to those in operation in jokes, are also frequently employed in dreams. Norbert's transformation of Gradiva into a marble relief 'is no more than an ingenious and poetical representation of the real event' (pp. 59–60 of Freud).

Thus it is hardly surprising that Jensen's text should privilege ambiguous language. Such language predominates whenever the most archaic processes are at work, the primary processes of the unconscious which pay no heed to contradiction and the logic of reason.[33] Several dreams are recounted in the story and one of its protagonists is suffering from a delusion. Nevertheless, ambiguous language is not proper to Norbert alone. Zoe, 'whose personality shows the most lucid clarity of mind', also makes abundant use of ambiguous language. Is this because she is given to punning? What is the status of ambiguous language in the discourses of the two main characters? According to Freud, Jensen makes a distinction between Norbert's discourse, which is unintentionally ambiguous, and Zoe's which, at first sight, seem intentionally ambiguous. Norbert is sick not because he speaks or understands double but because he uses the language of science, an apparently univocal, unambiguous language. A dead language, detached from any referant: the language of one who is deaf to desire. Norbert is able to grasp only the conscious, literal sense of language; he is 'led astray by a metaphor'.[34] He is under a misapprehension, one that is inevitable given the conflict, the rupture between his conscious and unconscious desires. Dissociating the signifier from the repressed signified, the proper or literal sense from the figurative, Norbert betrays his sickness by the loss of a function of language: the ability to invent metaphors, to indulge in word play, to catch the double meaning of a word or phrase without misunderstanding it. Someone who can no longer play with language, but who instead is unwittingly played *by* language, is sick.[35] Thus Norbert sets out for Pompeii to see whether he can find any 'trace' of Gradiva (p. 17 of Freud, p. 50 of Jensen). By 'trace' he understands the material imprint of her foot, since she has such an idiosyncratic manner of walking. Likewise he dreams of her sitting in the sun. The dream indicates clearly, in black and white, where the young girl is to be found. Yet, once again, one must know how to read, how to seize the different senses in a single expression, how to go beyond the literal meaning of the text:

> Hanold's discovery . . . is fully announced in the dream, but so cleverly concealed that it is bound to be overlooked. It is hidden, behind a play upon words, an ambiguity: somewhere in the sun Gradiva was sitting . . . And was not the

> 'somewhere' ... made to sound so hypocritically indefinite precisely because it introduced a definite piece of information about the place where Gradiva was staying? (p. 81 of Freud)

To be cured is to understand that the 'trace' is also the sign of a lost object, his childhood friend or his mother, and that the sun is also the name of an unknown or forgotten inn. It is to rediscover the polysemous nature of language and the childhood ability to play with words. This is what the end of the story signifies, when Norbert, now cured of his sickness, asks Zoe to cross over the paving stones ahead of him in the sunlight. A smile of complicity passes over her lips. As in the past, they are once more able to play with one another, to understand one another implicitly. To be able to communicate, to understand another person, involves using the art of double meanings. And it is because the 'most lucid' Zoe is expert in this art and makes strategic use of it that she is able to undertake Norbert's cure. The novelist gives Zoe a double language, an echo of Norbert's, which is designed to serve as a verbal bridge between conscious and unconscious: 'the author ... at this point [lends us] his powerful assistance. He puts the very same play on words into the girl's mouth when the next day she saw the metal clasp: "Did you find it in the sun, perhaps, which produces things of this kind?"' (p. 82 of Freud).

Here, Zoe plays the role of the analyst.

> In the course of the psychotherapeutic treatment of a delusion or an analagous disorder, ambiguous speeches of this kind are often produced by the patient, as new symptoms of the briefest duration, and it can happen that the doctor finds himself too in a position of making use of them. In that way it not infrequently happens that with the meaning that is intended for the patient's conscious he stirs up an understanding of the meaning that applies to the unconscious. I know from experience that the part thus played by ambiguity is apt to raise the greatest objection in the uninitiated and to give rise to the greatest misunderstandings. (pp. 85–6 of Freud)

What distinguishes Zoe from Norbert is that she is fully conscious of her use of ambiguous terms like those which symbolize repression:

> [this] perfect similarity between the burial of Pompeii – the disappearance of the past combined with its preservation – and repression, of which he [Hanold] possessed a knowledge through what might be described as 'endopsychic' perception. In this he was employing the same symbolism that the author makes the girl use unconsciously towards the conclusion of the story. (p. 51 of Freud)

Zoe's double meaning, her double science, intervenes at the moment when the hero's crisis reaches its climax, when he too is on the way to recovering a double ear. Dizzy and reeling from the effects of the sun and wine, he is drawn towards Gradiva by a dual feeling,[36] he begins to wonder about her 'bodily nature', he is hesitant, uneasy, anxious:[37] double effect of the double, uncanny effect which heralds the return of the repressed:

> So the author shows us his hero after his flight from love in a kind of crisis, in a state of complete confusion and distraction, in a turmoil such as we usually find at the climax of an illness, when neither of the two conflicting powers has any longer a sufficiently superior strength over the other for the margin between them to make it possible to establish a vigorous mental regime. But here the author intervenes helpfully and smoothes things out by making Gradiva appear at this juncture and undertake the cure of the delusion. (p. 69 of Freud)

Norbert is all the more overwhelmed by the crisis given that he has such a highly critical mind: it is this critical faculty that leads him, by an inevitable psychic process, to crisis point. It is his critical nature that makes him undertake an investigation of Gradiva's manner of walking (p. 17 of Jensen, p. 12 of Freud). He vents all his critical scorn on the absurdity of the honeymooning couples en route for Italy (pp. 29–30 of Jensen) and on Zoe's father, who travels so far to do something he could just as easily do at home (p. 74 of Jensen, p. 23 of Freud). No-one and nothing is spared his criticism, except himself. He needs the cure Zoe undertakes both to silence the overwhelming voice of his superego and to resolve his crisis: the latter is already a step towards the recovery of his health, but confusion and indecision can also act as an escape from reality, a means of remaining in a state of misunderstanding.[38]

To overcome his crisis means recovering the ability to hear, to understand others and himself. It is to opt for a clear meaning even if the condition for reaching clarity is to pass through ambiguity. To have 'lucid clarity of mind' is to have a double understanding, to have the double 'science' but to use it in the service of 'true' understanding against all misunderstandings. It is necessary to invent verbal bridges to show the imprint of the unconscious disguised by the pseudo-clarity of conscious discourse and to cure negative hallucinations. But ambiguous language seems to have only a strategic and didactic value for Freud. Is not Freud's ideal, after having established the links between the conscious and the unconscious, to put an end to all equivocity? To replace each element of the manifest text of the dream, delusion or novel by its latent content?

> But if this discovery [of the latent dream thoughts] could have become conscious, it would have meant the end of the delusion. Are we perhaps under an obligation to replace each separate piece of the manifest content of the dream by unconscious thoughts? Strictly speaking, yes; if we were interpreting a dream that had really been dreamt, we could not avoid that duty. But in that case too, the dreamer would have to give us the most copious explanations. Clearly we cannot carry out this requirement in the case of an author's creation. (p. 60)

It is worth noting, however, that Zoe, who plays the role of therapist, continues to use an ambiguous discourse. Does this mean she is not a perfect analyst? Is it not rather a way of showing that one must not make too rigid a division between the two protagonists, one the patient and the other the 'lucid' therapist, one duped by his unconscious, the other perfectly in control of her language? The strategy of using double meanings is perhaps not completely intentional. Zoe does not use ambiguity for purely therapeutic reasons. Her language can be interpreted as a series of tendentious word plays by which she indirectly gives vent to the erotic or aggressive desires she feels towards Norbert and her father. The pun allows her to make a saving of psychic expenditure, to obtain a pleasure that is a substitute for the pleasure which has been denied her in reality. Thus when she compares Norbert to an archaeopteryx, she invents a compromise in which thoughts of her friend's madness and that of her father (with whom she has identified Norbert) are fused. Archaeopteryx, the monstrosity 'which belongs to the archaeology of zoology' (p. 33 of Freud), a term which reveals all her resentment. Through her invention of ambiguous expressions Zoe reveals 'her therapeutic intentions and other secret designs as well' (p. 28 of Freud), which need to be deciphered. Zoe is also, to some extent, the dupe of her unconscious, and her language bears the trace of repressed desires, as the hurried way she speaks to the honeymooning friend she meets by chance in Pompeii shows. She replies to her friend's questions loudly and quickly and continues in her presence to adopt an equivocal language (pp. 91–2 of Jensen, pp. 27–8 of Freud). Zoe herself is not fully alive either (p. 102 of Jensen, p. 21 of Freud).

Thus Jensen's text, by its preference for ambiguous language, corroborates the Freudian interpretation. The ambiguity implies, more than a simple indetermination, the double determination of the discourse: it brings into play a conflict that takes place on a double scene. The author, by narrating a mystery, which is that of a delusion, accumulates the reasons for having to use a language of double meanings. Firstly, the structure of the narrative itself requires, if the story is to continue, that the mystery not be resolved immediately: the 'truth' must be unveiled little by little. Moreover, the double language is a corollary to the story's 'content': it is symptomatic of the psychic states of both protagonists.

There is a sort of complicity between the kind of narratives which involve the unveiling of a 'truth', whose narrations mimic the order of the real, which recounts events in relation to characters, and pschoanalytic interpretation; even if the latter contributes to the deconstruction of such a literature by showing that the author who makes such clever use of linguistic resources is able to do so only because he too is the dupe of his primary processes. As long as a text is called a 'fantasy' or a 'fiction', there will always be a decoder of riddles ready to reduce the fictional to the real.

Nevertheless, Jensen's text, even if it does authorize an analytic interpretation, also warns against dogmatic and reductive interpretations. In the novel, the character who represents the analyst, the character who holds, according to Freud, the key to the mystery, never reveals it in a language that is clear and rational. Until the end her language remains indecipherable and thus opposes, as if in advance, any translation of a poetic text into a univocal scientific language. There can be no analytic interpretation without countertransference: the analyst's unconscious, like everyone else's, cannot be eliminated. If analytic interpretation of a text reduces its undecidability, if it makes the text pass from obscurity to clarity, if it destroys the plurality of textual codes and favours one alone, then it is a 'dangerous supplement'. It remains a victim of the metaphysical opposition between the mad and the rational, poetry and science, conscious and unconscious. In this case, its claim to save the text from its delusion, to put it back on the straight and narrow by restoring a 'correct' understanding of it, is illegitimate. By making the text 'talk', it stops the play of writing.

Freud's reading, however nuanced, however polysemous it may be, however faithful it is intended to be (but perhaps we need to question the value of fidelity), by the fact that it accords Jensen's text the status of a manifest text whose latent content (which is its hidden truth) it aims to uncover – or, at best, construct – remains here a hermeneutic and thematic reading: in thrall to the metaphysical logos and its associated values; even if, simultaneously, this 'simple gloss' very seriously breaches the system of metaphysical oppositions and values.

The Double is/and the Devil
The Uncanniness of *The Sandman* (*Der Sandmann*)

For Serge Viderman

Thou shalt not make unto thee any graven image, or any likeness of any thing that is in heaven above, or that is in the earth beneath, or that is in the water under the earth.

Exodus 20, 4

Perhaps there is no more sublime passage in the Jewish Law than the commandment: 'Thou shalt not make unto thee any graven image' [etc.]

Kant, *The Critique of Judgement*, Book II

if it [art] abides by the formal aim of *mere imitation*, it provides not the reality of life, but only a pretence of life. After all, the Turks, as Mohammedans, do not, it is well known, tolerate any pictures of or copies of men, etc. James Bruce in his journey to Abyssinia showed paintings of a fish to a Turk; at first the Turk was astonished, but quickly enough he found an answer: 'If this fish shall rise up against you on the last day and say: "You have indeed given me a body but no living soul", how will you, then, justify yourself against this accusation?'

Hegel, *Introduction to Aesthetics*

For this same artisan is able to make not only all kinds of furniture but also all plants that grow from the earth, all animals including himself and, besides, the earth and the heavens and the gods, all things in heaven and all things in Hades below the earth ... This ... seems to me the most reasonable name to give him, namely that he is an imitator

> . . . Imitative art . . . is far removed from the truth, and that is why it seems it can make everything, because it touches only a small part of each thing, and that an image. The painter, if he should be a good painter . . . , he could deceive children and foolish men . . . some magician and imitator [who deceives them][1] into believing him all-wise.
>
> Plato, *The Republic*, Book X

The Double is/and the Devil
The Uncanniness of *The Sandman* (*Der Sandmann*)

Unity, multiplicity of the uncanny

The Uncanny – a text dominated by an investigation which is not, at any moment, complete without being immediately invalidated: in it the work of Eros is always undermined by the silent activity of the death instincts. Freud's stated desire is to arrive at the core of meaning proper to a concept, that of the *Unheimlich*, which would justify the use of a specific word.[2] A desire for the 'proper' which reduces the *Unheimlich* to a particular case of the *Heimlich*, by establishing a genetic relation between the derivation of the two terms. A desire which traces the different instances of *Unheimlichkeit* back to a single case: the uncanniness produced by the return of something familiar which ought to have remained secret, not to have revealed itself. This is according to Schelling's definition, which is the only one Freud pays attention to (cf. pp. 225–6 of *The Uncanny*). The enquiry is carried out in the hope of finding examples of uncanniness that everyone will accept without reserve. Freud confesses his own insensitivity in the matter: he himself has not experienced a feeling of uncanniness for a long time. Yet to carry out a successful investigation, great sensitivity to this quality of feeling would be more appropriate.[3] If we remember that in *The Moses of Michaelangelo* Freud takes as the point of departure for his analyses the powerful impression works of literature or the plastic arts make upon him,[4] we may well ask what motivates the desire for intelligibility in this case, since the usual motivation is lacking.

The study seems to have a polemical aim: professional writers on aesthetics ignore the subject of the uncanny, treating it as a mere side issue, only worthy of consideration in an appendix. It is precisely because traditional aesthetic approaches discard the uncanny, preferring to deal with 'what is beautiful, attractive and sublime – that is with feelings of a positive nature' than with 'the opposite feelings of repulsion and distress', that psychoanalysis must pay special attention to it.[5] Not to go beyond the empirical diversity of impressions and situations[6] that produce this type of feeling is to accept it as being of only secondary interest: for aestheticians, as for Freud, a feeling is only aesthetic if it is universally applicable. Freud's aim is thus to find cases which have uncanny effects on everyone, and at the same time to take into account individual variations in sensitivity. He would then have proved that writers on aesthetics are prisoners of metaphysical prejudices which lead to radical oppositions between the beautiful and the ugly, the attractive and the repulsive, the pleasant and the unpleasant etc. Moreover, the fact that negative feelings are ignored is an indication of their particular relevance to the psychoanalytic field of enquiry: psychoanalysis does not leave any remainders.

By picking out Schelling's definition from the numerous definitions of the *Unheimlich*, Freud shows that psychoanalysis has its contribution to make to the subject, since what is, in fact, at stake is a particular case of the return of the repressed. Moreover, Freud can thus hint at the inseparability of uncanny feelings and 'positive' aesthetic feelings: aesthetic pleasure itself also implies the return of repressed infantile fantasies. If this definition of the uncanny is not convertible, if not every instance of the return of the repressed provokes *Unheimlichkeit*, it remains nonetheless true that a radical opposition between 'positive' and 'negative' feelings becomes difficult to sustain. Better still: it is the aestheticians' 'debris' that helps to explain the nature of 'positive' aesthetic feelings. It seems that the difference between a work of art that causes pleasure and one that causes uncanniness is the degree to which the repressed content is 'disguised': one functions, so to speak, like a normal dream and the other like a nightmare. In the latter case there is a greater degree of recognition of the repressed than in the former – hence the dreamer's anxiety, proceeding from the superego's inability to accept such an explicit realization of desire.

All works of art would provoke feelings of uncanniness if artists did not use the seductive artifice of beauty to divert the ego's attention and prevent it from guarding against the return of repressed fantasies. The fore-pleasure produced by this seductive artifice covers up the 'negative' feeling just as it disguises the deeper pleasure confluent with it. In addition the 'negative feeling' is also, conversely, a source of pleasure: a pleasure from beyond the pleasure principle. *The Uncanny*, written a year before *Beyond the Pleasure Principle*, is set against a background of war,[7] death, the death instinct. The uncanny can also give rise to a masochistic type of pleasure, a satisfaction (*jouissance*) arising from the very source of anxiety itself; a pleasure which also leads back to the death instinct since it is linked to return and repetition. Thus, by extension, there is no aesthetic feeling in which the death instinct is not implicated. What traditional aesthetics wishes to disguise behind a rigid distinction between two types of feeling is that death is always already at work in the 'positive', that Eros and the death instinct are indissociable. Every pleasure is 'mixed'. Thus, by giving the uncanny more than marginal consideration, Freud 'uncannily' blurs the limits of the positive and negative.

Freud does not really say all this: he says it without saying it, implicitly. It is written on the reverse of the text:[8] the indissoluble union between Eros and the death instinct is inscribed within the Freudian text – itself particularly 'uncanny'.

In effect, the desire for unity which drives the investigation finds itself under attack at every turn from the need to introduce distinctions and divisions: even if, by several *tours de force*, Freud tries to erase these differences in favour of unity. Firstly there is a duality at the level of *method*: two types of analysis are used; a linguistic analysis of the notion of the *Unheimlich* and an analysis of all the properties, things, impressions, experiences and situations that give rise to *Unheimlichkeit*. A clever trick in presentation allows this duality to be reduced to unity and Freud to assert that the results of both analyses are identical: the order of exposition is not faithful to the order of invention. The linguistic analysis, which comes first, has, in fact, been carried out after the analysis of examples. The selection of linguistic material is determined by the latter which cannot, therefore, serve to confirm the results obtained by the linguistic method.

In the third part of the essay, Freud replies to a number of objections which threaten to destroy the unity he has obtained by these methods. The most important objection? That the proposed definition of the uncanny is not convertible: 'It may be true that the uncanny [*Unheimlich*] is something which is secretly familiar [*Heimlich-Heimisch*], which has undergone repression and then returned from it, and that everything that is uncanny fulfils this condition. But the selection of material on this basis does not enable us to solve the problem of the uncanny. For our proposition is clearly not convertible' (p. 245). A series of examples can, in effect, run counter to the psychoanalytic definition: all the themes used to support the hypothesis are capable of having different effects. Fairy tales, in particular, by situating themselves straight away in the realm of animism, the realm of the omnipotence of thoughts and desires, never give rise to feelings of uncanniness, despite the fact that they make frequent use of motifs considered to be particularly uncanny. Another objection: it is difficult to dismiss the factor of uncertainty (decisive in Jentsch's definition) as 'negligible', given its prime importance in producing the uncanny feelings associated with death.

Despite these objections, Freud *wants* to retain the proposed definition without qualifications, without leaving any remainder for the aestheticians:

> It is evident therefore, that we must be prepared to admit that there are other elements besides those which we have so far laid down as determining the production of uncanny feelings. We might say that these preliminary results have satisfied *psychoanalytic* interest in the problem of the uncanny and that what remains (*das Rest*) probably calls for an *aesthetic* enquiry. But that would be to open the door to doubts about what exactly is the value of our general contention that the uncanny proceeds from something familiar which has been repressed. (p. 247)

The objections disappear once an initial distinction is introduced: between works of *fiction* and *real* life. Most of the examples which weaken the psychoanalytic hypothesis are taken from the realm of fiction. In real life, the uncanny depends on straightforward conditions and occurs in very few cases. All of these, without exception, confirm the Freudian hypothesis – providing that a new dichotomy is introduced, that two types of revenant, two types of disappeared, are distinguished; firstly, what has disappeared because it has been *surmounted* and, secondly, what has disappeared because it has been *repressed*. The *Unheimlich* of the first type is more easily overcome than that of the second: only a person who has not completely surmounted his or her primitive animistic beliefs in the omnipotence of thoughts etc., and thinks they find confirmation of their former beliefs in the real, is likely to experience this kind of uncanniness: individual variations in sensibility to *Unheimlichkeit* are thus explained. Very precise psychological conditions are involved: in order to experience a feeling of uncanniness 'we must not feel quite sure of our new beliefs.' By the same token, intellectual uncertainty is, indirectly, reintroduced. In real life, instances of uncanniness are usually produced by the return of what has been surmounted rather than by the return of repressed infantile complexes. In the latter case, what is in play is no longer material but psychic reality: in this case there is a return of the repressed after the effective repression of some psychic content and not the abolition of belief in the reality of this content. The distinction between these two types of uncanny is considered by Freud to be *theoretically* amongst the most important, even if it often no longer applies in real life, where their limits become blurred since 'primitive beliefs are most intimately connected with infantile complexes and are, in fact, based on them' (p. 249). Over and above the divisions, unity is thus reestablished.

The uncanny in fiction 'merits in truth a separate discussion' (p. 249). It includes every instance of the uncanny that occurs in real life and more besides: a fictional supplement that psychoanalysis must take into account and by which it does not want to be outdone.[9] Here the distinction between two types of *Unheimlichkeit* cannot be upheld without qualifications:

> For the realm of phantasy depends for its effect on the fact that its content is not submitted to reality testing. The somewhat paradoxical result is that *in the first place a great deal that is not uncanny in fiction would be so if it happened in real life: and in the second place that there are many more means of creating uncanny effects in fiction than there are in real life.* (p. 249, Freud's italics)

From this there follows a further distinction: between works of fiction whose conventions admit animistic beliefs and those which claim to situate themselves in the realm of everyday reality. Works of the first kind would not produce uncanny feelings because there would be no conflict over whether 'things which have been "surmounted" and are regarded as incredible may not, after all, be possible' (p. 250). The key example: fairy tales. However, this is not self-evident and we can ask ourselves whether here Freud is not, in fact, revealing a 'predilection for smooth solutions and lucid expositions'. In effect, his line of argument could be that of a rationalist who is unaware of the full extent of unconscious forces and has not yet surmounted his belief in the omnipotence of judgement and reason: 'In fairy stories feelings of fear – including therefore uncanny feelings – are ruled out altogether. We understand this, and that is why we ignore any opportunities we find in them for developing such feelings' (p. 252). 'We adapt our judgement to the imaginary reality imposed on us by the writer ... In this case too we avoid all trace of the uncanny' (p. 250).

When the author of a work adopts realist conventions, everything that in real life gives rise to feelings of uncanniness has the same effect in the fictional work. This effect is, however, intensified by the poetic licence granted the writer to include 'events which never or rarely happen in fact' (p. 250). But if all fiction, as fiction, is not subject to reality-testing,[10] the preceding distinction becomes arbitrary: consequently the uncanny effect produced in this case is not pure; the reader is mystified and resents the author for 'in a sense, betraying us to the superstitiousness which we have ostensibly surmounted; he deceives us by promising to give us the sober truth and then after all overstepping it' (p. 251). The way for the writer to avoid incurring the reader's resentment? To keep him or her in the dark for as long as possible about 'the precise nature of the presuppositions on which the world he writes about is based' (ibid.).

Uncanniness which is produced by the return of repressed complexes is, in fiction, as in life, the most resistant case: it is the only case that is recognized by everyone without reservation. Thus Freud's reply to the objections allows him to uphold both the universality of uncanny effects and the existence of individual variations in experience. The reason he considers the distinction between these two types of 'revenant' to be so theoretically important is because it is this distinction alone that allows him to turn a feeling considered to be negative and negligible into one that is universal while at the same time preserving the singularity of individual instances.

It remains to show more precisely what distinguishes negative from positive pleasure if both, when they are universal, stem from the return of repressed infantile complexes. *The Uncanny* confines itself to general reflections on the writer's quasi-magical power to obtain different effects from the same material, carrying along a docile reader along in his or her wake. This power is the only condition that remains to distinguish between instances of uncanniness in real life and in fiction when they stem from the second type of return:

> We have clearly not exhausted the possibilities of poetic licence and the privileges enjoyed by story writers in evoking or excluding an uncanny feeling. In the main we adopt an unvarying, passive attitude towards real experience and are subject to the influence of our physical environment. But the story teller has a peculiarly directive power over us; by means of the moods he can put us into, he is able to guide the current of our emotions, to dam it up in one direction and make it flow in another, and he often obtains a great variety of effects from the same material. (p. 251)

In fiction the emotional effect is thus independent of the chosen subject matter: the same motif can produce either fear or laughter. It may provoke the first in the hero, the second in the reader: if the writer makes the hero look ridiculous or describes him satirically, the reader cannot identify with him.

The impasses of a thematic reading: the example of *The Sandman*

If, in the polemic that divides Freud and writers on aesthetics, we easily side with Freud, his demonstration remains nevertheless unconvincing, since the final remarks of the essay have the effect of invalidating his results. If it is possible to obtain a variety of different effects from the same material, it becomes impossible to draw any conclusions about the effects from the theme. Taking most of his examples from fiction, Freud does not take into account the specificity of this realm, a specificity which is subsequently acknowledged. His aim being to prove the existence of themes capable of producing a universal feeling of uncanniness, he makes a strictly thematic reading of the texts he sites as proof of his hypothesis. His reading of *The Sandman* is exemplary in this sense, and all the more revealing given that it is designed to serve as a paradigm for all cases of the same type: those in which the *Unheimlichkeit* is produced by the return of repressed infantile complexes, the most resistant cases, which are universally recognized. *The Sandman* generates a 'pure' feeling of uncanniness because of the return of the castration complex. Freud's short summary, and selection, of the text is governed by this interpretation.[11] 'This short summary leaves us in no doubt, I think, that the feeling of something uncanny is directly attached to the figure of the sandman, that is, to the idea of being robbed of one's eyes.'

'We shall venture therefore to refer the uncanny effect of the sandman to the anxiety belonging to the castration complex of childhood' (p. 233). Freud sees little point in differentiating between the uncanny effects of *The Sandman* and the tragic effects produced by the Oedipus story in which the same 'theme' occurs and which he mentions to justify the – rapid – passage from the fear of losing one's eyes to the fear of castration:

> We know from psychoanalytic experience, however, that the fear of damaging or losing one's eyes is a terrible one in children. Many adults retain their apprehensiveness in this respect and no physical injury is so much dreaded by them as an injury to the eye . . . A study of dreams, phantasies and myths has taught us that anxiety about one's eyes, the fear of going blind, is often enough a substitute for the dread of being castrated. The self-blinding of the mythical criminal, Oedipus, was simply a mitigated form of the punishment of castration – the only punishment that was adequate for him by the *lex talionis*. (p. 231)

With the example of *The Sandman* Freud *wants*, above all, to preserve the possibility of a 'pure' case which, by means of a fundamental theme, would always produce uncanniness. Its purity would distinguish *The Sandman* from Hoffmann's *The Devil's Elixir* [*Die Elixire des Teufels*][12] in which numerous motifs combine to produce a sense of uncanniness: a novel so dense and intricate that Freud decides against giving an extract from it (the 'resistance' of a text to summary, a function of its thematic plurality but also, perhaps, of its irreducibility to a thematic reading).

The analytic interpretation of *The Sandman* stands in opposition to Jentsch's reading in which the effects obtained depend essentially on the 'intellectual uncertainty' to which the Olympia episode gives rise: the conflict of judgement as to whether the 'doll' is a living or an inanimate being. Freud must exclude such a reading, which would classify the text among cases stemming from the first type of revenant (those in which the effect is produced by the return of beliefs that have not been completely 'surmounted'), since it means *The Sandman* could neither be at the origin of a universal feeling nor be used as a paradigm.

To be able to classify the text among examples of the second type, Freud must show that 'intellectual uncertainty' plays a negligible role. This would be the case if the impression *The Sandman* creates were derived, essentially, from the return of the infantile fear of castration: 'Jenstsch's point of an intellectual uncertainty has nothing to do with the effect. Uncertainty whether an object is living or inanimate, which admittedly applied to the doll Olympia, is quite irrelevant in connection with this other more striking instance of uncanniness' (p. 230). An 'intellectual uncertainty' regarding the literary genre is equally ruled out. If Freud does recognize that doubt is possible in this case, that it seems even to have been created intentionally by the author (which would be enough to classify *The Sandman* as a case of the first type, or at least as an 'impure' case), it is only to reassert immediately that any such doubt disappears as the story unfolds and that the conclusion is enough to remove any misconceptions:

> It is true that the writer creates a kind of uncertainty in us at the beginning by not letting us know, no doubt purposely, whether he is taking us into the real world or a purely fantastic one of his own creations . . . But this uncertainty disappears in the case of Hoffmann's story, and we perceive that he intends to make us, too, look through the demon optician's spectacle or spy-glass – perhaps, indeed, that the author in his very own person once peered through such an instrument. For the conclusion of the story makes it quite clear that Coppola the optician really is the lawyer Coppelius and also, therefore, the sandman. There is no question therefore of any intellectual uncertainty here: we know now that we are supposed to be looking on at the products of a madman's imagination, behind which we, with the superiority of rational minds, are able to detect the sober truth; and yet this knowledge does not lessen the impression of uncanniness in the least degree. The theory of intellectual uncertainty is thus incapable of explaining that impression. (pp. 230–1)

But why would the sandman and the fear of castration he awakens be a more significant example of uncanniness than the Olympia doll? The first argument, which today may seem bizarre, but which is necessarily bound up with a thematic type of interpretation, is the title, which dominates the whole text from on high and indicates its centre:[13] 'The main theme of the story is, on the contrary, something different, something which gives it its name and which is always reintroduced at critical moments: it is the theme of the "Sand-man" who tears out children's eyes' (p. 227).[14]

The other, more serious, argument, the only one which refers to the 'form'[15] of the story, is to say that the Olympia episode could not produce an uncanny effect since it is given a satirical treatment:

> But I cannot think – and I hope most readers of the story would agree with me – that the theme of the doll Olympia, who is to all appearances a living being, is by any means the

> only, or indeed the most important, element that must be held responsible for the quite unparalleled atmosphere of uncanniness evoked by the story. Nor is this atmosphere heightened by the fact that the author himself treats the episode with a faint touch of satire and uses it to poke fun at the young man's idealisation of his mistress. (p. 227)

In fact, if we read Hoffmann's story and not just Freud's summary of it, we may begin to wonder whether the satirical element comes into play only at this level of the story (in which, moreover, it is used sparingly and to definite purpose); whether the intellectual uncertainty about genre is really resolved at the end of the story; whether the uncanniness produced by the Olympia doll and the sandman are really of different kinds and whether it *is* possible to separate the two themes. Freud's conclusions are the outcome of a thematic interpretation which makes a false economy on the specificity of fiction and the story's narrative structure. In *The Sandman*, the narrative structure is particularly complex and inseparable from the 'themes' explored.

The writer's eye-glass: the imaginary and the real

The complexity of the tale: it begins with an exchange of letters between Nathaniel, Lothario and Clara (two characters to whom Freud pays hardly any attention); it continues with a direct address by the author to the reader; finally it unfolds according to the most banal narrative conventions. The presence of several characters who have very different perspectives on Nathaniel's story from his own, a point of view that is at times contradictory, at times satirical, helps to prolong the 'intellectual uncertainty' until the very end of the story. If Nathaniel's fiancée Clara's perspective is, as her name suggests, 'clear', simple, realist; if her point of view is also shared by her brother Lothario, and the rest of the entourage, a sensible and reasonable point of view that contrasts with Nathaniel's – Nathaniel the dreamer, the visionary, the madman who confuses the imaginary and the real, who sees double – it is nonetheless not described as the perspective that contains the truth, and the reader can no more identify with Clara than with Nathaniel. Moreover, Hoffmann's treatment of the realist perspective is tinged with irony and it seems as if he inclines more towards the visionary perspective, which is also his own. Yet this is not presented as being a 'true' perspective either. The fact that the conclusion of the story seems to endorse Nathaniel's version of events is not decisive: what happens here is perhaps an 'uncanny' coincidence between fantasy and reality. But above all, contrary to what Freud says, the ending remains ambiguous and the reader's doubts are not resolved. Freud's summary says that Clara, from the top of the tower where she and Nathaniel have climbed, sees a curious object moving along the street. Nathaniel examines this object through Coppola's spy-glass and, on recognizing Coppelius,[16] is seized by a fit of madness. In Hoffmann's version, all that is described is the approach of an indistinct form, sufficiently vague for everyone to project their own fantasies onto it: 'Then the loving pair ... gazed out at the fragrant woodland and at the blue mountains that rose like a giant city beyond. "Just look at that funny little grey bush that seems as if it is coming towards us"'[17] Nathaniel takes the spy-glass from his pocket and, more than the appearance of Coppola, it is the use of this telescope that triggers off his madness. Through the spy-glass, it is the face of Clara, the fiancée he thought that he would finally be able to marry, which appears terrifying to him, a veritable Medusa's head, as he imagined her in his poem. This is why he tries to throw her off the tower: 'Nathaniel reached into his side-pocket; he found Coppola's telescope and gazed through it. Clara was standing before the glass! Then a spasm shuddered through him; pale as death, he stared at Clara' (p. 123). 'Nathaniel looked into Clara's eyes, but it was death which gazed at him mildly out of them' (p. 105, end of the poem).

Through a spy-glass one's view of the real can only be

deformed. The German word is: *Perspektiv*. The different characters the writer creates are so many different perspectives on the real. Even the eye of the person who sees clearly is a lens or a telescope. Coppola, the spectacle dealer, calls his spectacles 'lovely eyes'. One eye does not see more truthfully than another, even if one eye is never the same (or as good) as another: certain perspectives can be worth more than others, one leading to a happy marriage (hence Clara's 'happy-end'),[18] another to madness and death; but neither can be more truthful. What seems interesting and *unheimlich* in Hoffmann's text (which is Nietzschean *avant la lettre*) is that it shows that it is not a case of madness on one side and reason on the other but that their limits are not clearly defined, each being a matter of perspective. A blurring of the limits between the normal and the pathological, the imaginary and the real, that places *The Sandman* among works producing uncanny effects of the first type rather than the second. But polemics prevents Freud from recognizing this: faced with Hoffmann's intentional undecidability, he opts for Nathaniel's point of view: the reader is not, he says, the superior and rational person he or she thinks. Without a doubt. But this does not mean that Nathaniel's visions are not the product of 'fantasy'.

The shifting of fixed margins and limits seems, for Hoffmann, to be literature's essential function. It is the artist's privilege not to imitate a pre-existing reality, but to represent the real through a multiplicity of distorting eye-glasses, each constitutive of a different reality. In a work of fiction, each of the characters is an external projection of the artist's multiple visions. Freud knew that Hoffmann considered his fictional characters to be images derived from impressions received before the age of two years and preserved in the camera obscura of his unconscious until they were later developed.[19]

For Hoffmann, writing is a painting which refers back to an internal, not an external, model. The aim of writing is to create lifelike portraits without needing to refer to the original to judge whether the likeness is a good one: an originary double which always already doubles perception, tinging the real with madness:

> Perhaps, like a good portrait painter, I shall succeed in catching more than one figure in such a way that, although you never knew its original, you will nevertheless think it lifelike, that you had indeed seen the person many times with your living eyes. Perhaps you will then come to believe, O reader, that there is nothing more marvellous or madder than real life, and that all the poet could do was catch this as a dark reflection caught on a dull mirror. (p. 101)

Thus the portrait of Clara does not correspond to the description of a real model, but is presented as a collection of points of view: Clara merges with the series of perspectives that various lenses have upon her and which more or less intersect: artists' lenses which always reproduce the reality of their particular visions:

> Clara could not possibly be called beautiful: that was the opinion of all those whose office it was to understand beauty. But if the architects lauded the perfect proportions of her figure, if the painters found her neck, her shoulders, and breast almost too chastely formed, all were enamoured of her wonderful Magdalen hair and babbled about her complexion. One of them, however, a real visionary, had the very strange notion of comparing Clara's eyes with a lake of Ruisdael with the pure azure of a cloudless sky, woodland and flowery meadow, the whole motley life of a rich landscape reflected in them. Poets and musicians, however, went further and said "What lake, what reflection? When we behold her, we hear heavenly tones streaming towards us from out of her eyes . . . If we are not then inspired to any truly accomplished song, that is because we are in general of very little account, and that is the fact we read unmistakeably in the smile that plays about Clara's mouth." (pp. 101–2)

Clara's superiority over Nathaniel lies in the fact that she realizes that everything is a matter of perspective: every point of view is exactly that: making him see reason, for her, is convincing him that his external vision reflects an internal reality.

Nathaniel's 'madness' is subject to the same processes as Hoffmann's notion of literary 'creation': both are subject to an inner compulsion attributed to an external force:

> he spoke continually of how each of us, thinking himself free, was in reality the tortured plaything of mysterious powers: resistance was vain; we had humbly to submit to the decrees of fate. He went so far as to assert that it was folly to think the creations of art and science the product of our own free will: the inspiration which alone made creation possible did not proceed from within us but was effectuated by some higher force from outside. (p. 103)

A strong inner compulsion which obliges the author to describe to others his bizarre, magnificent, terrifying visions in glowing colours but without finding words that are adequate to the task: 'every word, everything capable of being spoken seemed ... colourless and cold and dead' (p. 100). A discrepancy between the dead and deadly word and the fiery vitality of the vision that explains the structural complexity of the story.[20] Hoffmann first of all sketches a rough outline of his inner vision – the letters at the beginning of the story. He then adds more and more glowing colours to reproduce as faithfully as possible 'the picture ... come forth [from his] heart'. The only reason that the expression of the vital vision, an expression which his 'strong compulsion ... to speak about Nathaniel's unhappy life' necessitates, is expressed in writing rather than verbally is the absence of a listener.

But why should this initial sketch take the form of an exchange of letters? In what sense is the letter of a letter different from that of a direct narrative mode? For Hoffmann the epistolary mode is decisive at this point to get the reader to accept the fantastical account which follows, which is 'as much as a poet [can] do'. Thus it is really the form of the narrative and not the theme in itself which plays the decisive role in the production of effects.[21] In order to create an effect of uncanniness right from the beginning, this beginning must be striking, original and gripping. This excludes any beginning that is too prosaic: 'Once upon a time', or one that is likely to create a comic effect ('Go to the devil! cried the student Nathaniel'). Beginning with an exchange of letters avoids the problem of finding the right beginning since, in effect, it is 'not to begin at all' (pp. 100–1). There can be no instance of the uncanny that does not always already imply repetition. Moreover, what the letter expresses, not literally but implicitly, on the reverse of the text,[22] is what is proper to writing itself: the letter of writing literally never begins but is always a repetition of an originary repetition, a double and thus triple writing: the exchange of three letters. And it continues. Writing's supplementarity indefinitely calls forth supplementarity because there has never been an originary model perfectly present and complete, because without writing the inner visions in all their 'colours and light and shade' remain vague, indefinite, evanescent. If these visions were so glorious, so vivid, why would there be any need to resort to a double regarded as inferior and deadly? Mimesis is necessary and originary because life always already implies death and needs the mortal supplement to be fixed and take form. Hoffmann does not really say all this: while rejecting a mimesis that is the double of a pre-existing external reality, he seems to suppose the existence of an internal vital reality which serves as a model. On the other hand, death is originarily inscribed within his text, by the very fact that it begins with the absence of a beginning. The necessity of writing and not just of narrating out loud is essential; writing is not a mere substitute for speech. It indicates that life must necessarily always pass through death. Thus Nathaniel wonders why he writes down his childhood memories in a letter to Lothario instead of recounting them to him on his imminent return home: 'But why am I writing you all this? I could have told you about it better and at greater length face to face – for you must now learn that I shall be with you in a fortnight's time.'

The fact that Nathaniel's letters contain childhood memories, and particularly terrifying ones at that, is of equal significance in explaining why writing is privileged over speech. The written word fixes more surely than the spoken; in addition, Nathaniel's letter affords him the masochistic pleasure of reliving his past once more, detail by detail, narcissistically, without the fear of being disturbed by anyone, of being interrupted by his fiancée's 'prosaic' comments or the sensible Clara's possible objections. Yet, nevertheless, a letter is meant to be read, even if it does not reach its destinee. Nathaniel, who has written his letter to Lothario, commits the very significant parapraxis of sending it to Clara. Masochistic pleasure is the reverse side of his sadism: by his letter he aims to frighten and persecute Clara, to break their engagement, to cause suffering and death.

Moreover, it could be said that through writing Nathaniel constructs rather than recollects his memories: it is impossible to distinguish the narrative of his childhood memories from that of his fantasies, the tale of the past from the imagined story of the future. The narration of his childhood memories is already literature, just as the fictional poem in which he imagines his future is a self-punishing repetition of the past. The function of both is the same: firstly, to rekindle in glowing colours what has already begun to fade from the imagination: 'The figure of the repulsive Coppelius had, as Nathaniel himself was constrained to admit, grown dim in his imagination, and in his tales, where Coppelius appeared as a malign agent of destiny; it often required an effort to bestow life and colour upon him' (pp. 104–5). Secondly, to enable him to master, by symbolically repeating them, his terrifying visions; to master the future by predicting it, but also, sadomasochistically, to anticipate it, since the future he imagines will, in fact, be realized in an amazing coincidence between fantasy and reality:

> At length he hit on the idea of making his gloomy foreboding that Coppelius would disrupt the joy of his love into the subject of a poem: he depicted himself and Clara as united in true love but now and then it was as if a black hand reached out over them and erased their feelings of joy; at last, as they were standing before the marriage altar, the terrible Coppelius appeared and touched Clara's lovely eyes, which sprang out like blood-red sparks, singeing and burning onto Nathaniel's breast. Coppelius then seized him and threw him into a flaming circle of fire [etc . . .]. While Nathaniel was composing his poem he was very quiet and self-possessed: he polished and improved every line, and the constraint of metre made it possible for him not to rest until everything was clear and harmonious. Yet when he had finished the poem and read it aloud to himself, he was seized with horror, and exclaimed: 'Whose dreadful voice is this?!' Before long, however, it again seemed to him no more than a good poem, and he came to think that Clara's cold disposition would certainly be inflamed by it, although at the same time he had no clear notion of what Clara's becoming inflamed might lead to or of what purpose could be served by distressing her with horrible images prophesying a terrible destiny and the destruction of their love. (pp. 105–6)

Nathaniel's literary activity, which implicitly illuminates Hoffmann's own, is inseparable from the other 'themes' of the story, those of the sandman and the fear of losing one's eyes. It is significant that literature is conceived as painting, as a *visionary* literature. Nathaniel's literary activity is inseparable from his relations with women: what he seeks in a woman, whether it is Clara or Olympia, is a docile and passive listener for his poems: a strictly narcissistic pleasure: 'From the profoundest depths of his writing desk, Nathaniel fetched up everything he had ever written: poems, fantasies, visions, novels, tales, daily augmented by random sonnets, short stanzas, canzoni, and he read them all to Olympia without wearying for hours on end. And he had never before had so marvellous an auditor' (p. 117). An overwhelming literary output which repeats the symbolic activity he carried out as a child during the periods when Coppelius did not visit his father: when he would draw pictures of the sandman in numerous different forms: 'On tables, cupboards, and walls everywhere in the house . . . the strangest and most hideous pictures' (p. 88).

Not only does this activity enable him to master his terror of the sandman by drawing derisory caricatures of him,[23] it is also a means of masochistic self-torture: a pleasure stemming from beyond the pleasure principle, one that is highly prized by our hero. While the sandman is a hideous, terrifying, anguishing, *unheimlich* figure whose presence he consciously flees, unconsciously he desires it. At night he summons the sandman back in his dreams: 'When I heard the sound of clumping coming up the stairs in the evening I trembled with fear and terror . . . I was the first to run into the bedroom on the nights he was coming, and his fearsome apparition tormented me till dawn' (p. 87).

Nathaniel's extreme taste for tales of witches, goblins and evil creatures of all kinds, and the fact that he prefers his nurse's sadistic account of the sandman to his mother's more reassuring version, also stems from the same pleasure in the negative. The perception of the real is always anticipated by him in an ill-fated form: the fantasized double doubles the real, gives it its particular colouring: thus when Nathaniel, hoping to catch a glimpse of the sandman, discovers only the lawyer Coppelius, he endows him with all the sandman's terrifying features and creates a picture of him that could not possibly correspond to any real being. 'The sandman, the terrible sandman, was the aged advocate Coppelius, who sometimes comes to lunch with us. But the most horrible of forms could not have aroused in me a more profound terror than did this Coppelius' (p. 89).

Fantasy and reality coincide because reality is always structured by fantasy, because it has never been present as such. Thus it is impossible to establish fixed, definite boundaries between the real and the imaginary: a blurring of distinctions that is particularly likely to produce uncanniness, according to Freud (cf. p. 244 of *The Uncanny*).

A reading of *The Sandman* cannot therefore ignore the presence of repetition and doubling in all its multiple forms, which is an important factor in producing an impression of uncanniness. If the fear of losing one's eyes reinforces this effect, then it cannot perhaps be dissociated from the effect of doubling, from Nathaniel's fantasies and literary activity. There is no need to refer to the general symbolism of dreams and myths to understand the anxiety Hoffmann's text arouses if we take into account not one theme in isolation but the way it is connected with the others. Thus the Olympia episode and its effect is inseparable from the uncanny effect produced by the sandman and also from the problem of the double.

The animate and the inanimate: diabolical mimesis

For Freud the uncanny effect produced by the Olympia episode is in some sense negligible. The impossibility of deciding whether she is animate or inanimate produces only limited uncertainty and the uncanny impression which is puduced by this uncertainty is very different from the uncanniness of the rest of the text. In fact, the doll is only another form of the double and the uncertainty she creates can hardly be distinguished from that produced by literature and painting as doubles. As imitations, the latter also create an illusion of life. Thus Nathaniel, through the fatal power of writing, can make Clara burst into tears, terrify her merely by reading her his poems. Fiction has a greater effect on him than life, and gradually replaces it: from being a mere representation of life it ends up taking its place, bringing madness and death in its wake. Literature as a mimesis which becomes a substitute for life is a perversion belonging to the creature who rivals God: a diabolical mimesis.

The sensible Clara, who prefers life to its double, does not fall victim to the illusion, she does not confuse the animate and the inanimate: 'Fantasists enjoyed little success with her: for, although she did not say very much . . . her bright eyes and that subtle ironical smile told them: "Dear friends! How could you believe of me that I should regard your transient poetic fancies as real beings, possessing life and action?" For this reason Clara was stigmatised by many as cold, unfeeling, prosaic' (p. 102). In conformity with a whole philosophical tradition, Clara both rejects the double as inferior to life and distinguishes two types of mimesis: a bad mimesis whose effects are harmful and whose products carry the mark of the devil: they cause boredom and horror; and a good, divine mimesis which brings joy and life:

> In former days he had a great gift for lively and cheerful stories, which he would write down and Clara would listen to with the most heartfelt enjoyment; now his tales had grown gloomy, incomprehensible and formless, so that even if Clara considerately refrained from saying so he could nevertheless sense how little they appealed to her. Clara found boredom almost unendurable: when she was bored, the most unconquerable weariness of mind she felt appeared in how she spoke and in the look in her eyes. (p. 104)

Bad mimesis makes Nathaniel forget the living presence of Clara and turn instead to dead representatives. Nathaniel's perversion is illustrated by his indifference to Clara's charms, the fact that he prefers his dead fiancée to his flesh and blood one, and his failure to distinguish between the living and the dead. In the grip of the demonic power that has entered his life, all his values undergo a transmutation: he takes Clara for a 'lifeless, accursed automaton' (p. 106) and wants to marry Olympia. The Olympia episode cannot, therefore, be treated in isolation from the rest: it is the inverted image of Nathaniel's relationship with Clara, illustrating in capital letters the power the double exercises over the hero. Nathaniel prefers the automaton to the living woman because he flees the latter, with whom he could begin a sexually productive activity. What he wants is a frigid, lifeless woman, a mirror of himself, who will listen to his poems without growing weary: 'O lovely, heavenly woman! . . . O heart in which my whole being is reflected!' (p. 114). Nathaniel's narcissism makes him unfit for object-love, for forbidden love. The correlative of his narcissism is his 'creative' activity, the production of doubles, a substitute for procreation.

If, in an important note, Freud does mention Nathaniel's narcissism and sees in Olympia Nathaniel's double, he nonetheless does not develop this idea at all in terms of his general interpretation and, above all, he does not connect narcissism and doubling with literary 'creation'. In fact, it is Nathaniel's love for his 'creatures' that makes him confuse the animate and the inanimate: it is he himself who gives life to his works, who lends his *eyes* to his mirror-image.[24] Olympia's expressionless eyes come to life only when he reads her his poems: 'And he never before had so marvellous an auditor: she did not sew or knit, she did not gaze out of the window, she did not feed a cagebird, she did not play with a lapdog . . . She sat motionless, her gaze fixed on the eyes of her beloved with a look that grew ever more animated and more passionate' (p. 117).

Nathaniel brings Olympia to life at the expense of his own: Coppola can only create Olympia by stealing Nathaniel's eyes just as the sandman must tear out children's eyes in order to feed his own children.

Thus eyes, in Hoffmann's tale, are the life principle – but the principle of an arificial life: the hero can only create narcissistically through his eyes, not procreate through his genitals. It is not coincidental that his way of estranging Clara and breaking off his engagement is to read her his poems. If, in the story, the eye is a substitute for the sex, this must be understood literally and not symbolically. Nathaniel can only create by artificial means, by mimesis, by mimicking or doubling life: a power of representation, of vision, of divison which belongs to the death instincts, not to Eros. The eye is a diabolical source of life: a demonic power of doubling. Indeed, one could almost say the opposite to Freud, that for Nathaniel to lose his eyes would mean the recovery of his sex.

But Freud, who only takes the 'theme' of eyes into account in relation to the sandman episode, regards the fear of losing one's eyes as a symbolic substitute for the fear of castration: he sees the sandman as a substitute for the castrating father who always intervenes to spoil love. In this case a series of doublings must be recognized which stems from the son's ambivalence towards his father. The good father is represented by the figure of Nathaniel's father, the bad father by the sandman and the lawyer Coppelius. In turn, Coppola and Professor Spalanzani are two paternal figures – but at this point Freud's theory proves inadequate, since neither of the latter could fill the role of the good father: Spalanzani is Coppola's accomplice and is involved in manufacturing automata with him. The inadequacy of Freud's hypothesis is underlined by the fact that he is forced to assert that the death-wish against the 'bad' father is repressed and transferred onto the figure of the 'good' father with Coppelius as intermediary. But this ignores Nathaniel's desire to kill Coppelius, his attempt to strangle Spalanzani, and his desire to crush his rivals. Freud's over-simplistic schema forces him to see Coppelius' attempts to unscrew Nathaniel's arms and legs as another equivalent of castration. The only purpose of this – according to Freud – bizarre incident would thus be to show that Coppelius and his 'latter counterpart Spalanzani, the mechanician' are in fact one and the same, and to prove that Olympia represents the materialization of Nathaniel's passive attitude towards his father. Whatever the case, the episode is 'a singular feature, which seems quite outside the picture of the sandman'.

In fact Coppelius' gesture inscribes itself closely within this picture and loses its singularity once one accepts that the Olympia episode cannot be separated from that of the sandman.

Primal scene and satanic sorcery: the devil's artifices

When Coppelius tries to unscrew the child's arms and legs like a doll's, he speaks the 'mysterious' words which contain the key to all his strange machinations:

> And with that he seized me so violently that my joints cracked, unscrewed my hands and feet and fixed them on again, now in this way, now in that. 'They don't look right anywhere! Better where they were! The old one knew what he was doing!' Coppelius lisped and hissed. But everything went dark around me, a sudden spasm shot through my frame – I felt nothing move. A warm gentle breath passed across my face; I awoke as if from the sleep of death; my mother was bending over me. (pp. 91 – 2)[25]

Coppelius' words are those of a rival of God's (the old one) and express his anger at being unable to improve on God's work. To unscrew the boy's arms and legs is not to castrate him but to fragment a living unity by treating it like a machine: it is to want to recreate life from inert matter: a diabolical activity that is doomed to failure. The diabolical double is always already a work of death, always already dead. Nathaniel's fear of being broken up into separate parts is the fear of dying. Coppelius, Coppola and Spalanzani are all creators of artificial beings, charlatans, counterfeiters, God's imitators, Caligliostros all three of them. The activities Nathaniel's father carries out with Coppelius the lawyer, the sandman, are magical acts of sorcery in which fire and alchemical transformations play an important role. This accounts for the truly apocalyptic visions of Nathaniel's fantasy-poem and his final fit of madness, in which his fantasies of fragmentation and transformation by fire return:

> At this point Nathaniel saw that a pair of blood-flecked eyes were lying on the floor and staring up at him; Spalanzani seized them . . . and threw them at him, so that they struck him in the chest. Them madness gripped him with hot

> glowing claws, tore its way into him and blasted his mind: 'Ha, ha, ha! Circle of fire, circle of fire! Spin, spin, circle of fire! Merrily, merrily! Puppet, ha, lovely puppet, spin, spin!' (p. 120)

Wheel: 'form of torture in which after a prisoner had been broken he was tied to a wheel; term of alchemy. The Wheel of the elements used by the sages, the passage of time, a year's revolution: The conversion of the elements' (*Littré*).[26] The Wheel, instrument of the devil: 'I made the eyes! – I made the clockwork![27] – Devil! – Stop! – Puppet showman! – Beast!' (dialogue between Spalanzani and Coppola, p. 119).

Clara interprets the lawyer's mysterious visits to Nathaniel's house as part of a 'diabolical' commerce between him and Nathaniel's father. She attributes his father's death to the dangers involved in alchemical experiments and to his negligence[28] (thus putting an end to the split between the good and bad father and restoring his unbearable ambiguity):

> The uncanny night time activities with your father were no doubt nothing more than secret [*insgeheim*] alchemical experiments they were making together, and your mother could hardly have been pleased about it, since a lot of money was undoubtedly wasted and, with such laboratory experiments, your father, altogether absorbed in the deceptive desire for higher truth, would have become estranged from his own family. Your father surely brought about his own death through his own carelessness and Coppelius is not to blame for it. (p. 95; cf. also p. 100)

Unheimlich is also a term for the occult art of magic, for someone who is expert in occult and rare practices: Freud picks up this sense of the word but does not develop it.

The father's illusory desire is to create life from inanimate matter, to manufacture artificial beings. Spalanzani, Olympia's father, has almost the same name (but for one letter) as the Italian biologist, a contemporary of Hoffmann's, who carried out the first experiments in artificial insemination. Artificial insemination in which the eye, not the genitals is the source of life, underpinned by the seductive snare of narcissism, which deludes and deceives: the fertilization carried out by the sandman, who sows his seed 'wastefully' by sowing it in sand. A sowing of sand (*Sand*) not of sperm (*Same*), one sterile,[29] the other fertile, but for a couple of letters, identical seeds. Two seeds, just as there are two kinds of mimesis, one sowing the good grain, the other the bad. Also two kinds of seedbed: the sandman tears eyes from their sockets and transports them into other orbits – black (anal?) cavities (p. 91) which mimic, by simulacrum, the antrum, the mother's fertile womb. The diabolical act of creation, which 'wastes a lot of money', takes place between men: it can only be a creation from inanimate matter. But the devil's mistake is to try to pass off the inanimate for the living, trying to improve on nature by creating a perfect 'creature'.

It is precisely this perfection that appears suspect to the more observant characters in the story and prevents them falling into the same trap as Nathaniel.[30] Olympia is perfect: her features are admirably regular, her figure perfectly proportioned, the rhythm of her dancing singularly exact. But it is this very perfection that makes her seem strange: her stiff, unnatural, stilted, formal manner. In particular, her fixed, lifeless gaze[31] makes her appear rigid and soulless:

> every one of her movements seems as if controlled by clockwork. When she plays and sings it is with the unpleasant soulless regularity of a machine, and she dances in the same way. We have come to find this Olympia quite uncanny; we would like to have nothing to do with her; it seems to us that she is only acting like a living creature, and yet there is some reason for that which we cannot fathom. (p. 116)

This is how Olympia appears in most people's eyes, but not in Nathaniel's. When he looks at her he finds that he is finally in possession of himself: which is why Olympia is completely '*heimlich*' to him (cf. p. 115).[32]

Perfection is thus the sign that one is dealing with a machine which is mimicking life; an apparent perfection which both masks and reveals its connection with the powers of darkness, with the rigidity and coldness of death.[33] The icy coldness of Olympia's hand is reminiscent of Goethe's 'dead bride'. In *The Sandman*, deathly rigidity and fixity are the indications of a diabolical presence: every time Nathaniel's father is expecting a visit from Coppelius, he falls silent and becomes motionless (pp. 86 and 88).[34] Nathaniel feels 'as if crushed beneath a rock'.[35] At the sight of Coppola running off with Olympia over his shoulder, Nathaniel is struck dumb, paralysed with horror. Spying on the scene of the sorcerers' activities, he is rooted to the spot, as if bewitched. Finally, when he is reading his diabolical poems to Clara she too is frozen by his words (p. 106). The double is neither living nor dead: designed to supplement the living, to perfect it, to make it immortal like the Creator, it is always 'the harbinger of death'. It disguises, by its perfection, the presence of death. By creating what he hopes are immortal doubles, man tries to conceal the fact that death is always already present in life. The feeling of uncanniness that arises from the double stems from the fact that it cannot but evoke what man tries in vain to forget.

The scene which Nathaniel witnesses as a child from behind the curtain is especially *unheimlich* because it is the spectacle of an attempt to create life from inert matter; a vision capable of castrating whoever witnesses it, because it reveals the indissoluble bond between life and death. Thus Nathaniel can prefer artistic, narcissistic creation, producing doubles he thinks are immortal, to procreation. His artistic activity can therefore be interpreted as a consequence of this vision. But we can go even further: the sorcery scene mimics by simulacrum the primal scene, of which it cannot fail to remind us. Nathaniel is not a hidden witness, as he desires, at his own conception, but he is present at the conception of another being, a creation for which his eyes are necessary. The artificial creation of a double is thus reminiscent of the procreation of a sister or brother whose birth robs the child of something fundamental. Thus the spectacle can only give him a masochistic pleasure. There are several indications in the text to the effect that the sorcery scene is a diabolical reenactment of the primal scene. It always occurs at night, in ritualistic fashion, at the same time; it is linked with certain specific sounds – the heavy thudding steps of a man coming up the stairs and characteristic creakings. Most of its elements are inverted: it involves two men and results in an unnatural creation; the silent and motionless father plays a passive role. The two protagonists undress and put on black smocks rather than white ones – 'night' wear. It all takes place as if Nathaniel, anxious to possess the supreme knowledge of how children are created, finds the answer to his curiosity by fantasizing a Promethean type of magical creation from which women are excluded. A forbidden knowledge for which he will necessarily be punished. Nathaniel expects to be punished, he always already predicts it and awaits it in fear and trembling. At this point we should read the complete text:

> At the risk of being discovered and, as I firmly believed, severely punished, I remained there listening, with my head stuck through the curtains. My father received Coppelius solemnly. 'Up! To work!' Coppelius cried in a hoarse, growling voice, and threw off his coat. My father slowly and gloomily removed his dressing gown and both clad themselves in long black smocks. I did not see where they got them from. My father opened the folding doors of a wall-cupboard; but I saw that what I had for so long taken to be a wall-cupboard was, rather, a black cavern, in which there stood a small hearth. Coppelius approached it and a blue flame flickered upon the hearth. All kinds of strange implements lay around. Good God! As my father bent down to the fire, he looked quite different! A dreadful convulsive pain seemed to have distorted his gentle, honest features into

> a repulsive devil mask. He looked like Coppelius. The latter seized the glowing tongs and with them drew brightly glowing substances out of the thick black smoke and began vigorously to hammer away at them. I seemed to see human faces appearing all around, but without eyes – instead of eyes there were hideous black cavities. 'Eyes, bring eyes!' Coppelius cried in a dull, hollow voice. Gripped by wild terror, I screamed aloud and fell out of my hiding place onto the floor. (pp. 90–1)

The child's expectation that he will be punished could only be so strong because it evokes an earlier punishment, that punishment suffered, or fantasized, for having spied or having wanted to spy on the primal scene. The father would then have intervened and threatened the child with castration. The latter's present fear of losing his eyes is not a substitute for the fear of castration, but it cannot fail to evoke it: it is the self-punishing repetition of the fear of castration, in a more sadistic form, since it is linked to the loss of life and the fragmentation of a living whole. The sorcery scene is therefore the 'real' return of another scene which was perhaps only fantasized. But with the primitive fantasy always doubling present perception, it is difficult to distinguish what part each plays. In this case, what produces the uncanny is overdetermined: it is the sorcery scene, *unheimlich* in its own right because connected with the problem of the double; it is the return of the castration fantasy in the guise of the more anguishing fragmentation fantasy; but, above all, it is the coincidence of fantasy with the real.

Nevertheless, the return of castration fear can only come into play if we accept the primal scene as the latent content of the sorcery scene: a manifest text which in itself is enough to produce uncanniness: the impression is thus not a 'pure' one. Perhaps, as in real life, it is impossible to distinguish, except by an abstraction, between the effect produced by the return of repressed infantile complexes and that produced by the persistence of animistic beliefs. If Nathaniel is so horrified by the sight, by the fantasy of a magical kind of 'creation', it is perhaps because, during that other scene which can, hypothetically, be deduced from the manifest text of what actually took place, he himself experienced a desire for self-creation, a desire to take his father's place. The passive role attributed to the father in the actual scene would thus be a reprisal for the fear of castration the child experienced at that time for having wanted to take his father's place. The fact that in the actual scene the mother is replaced by Coppelius can be put down to repression and indicates a strong mother fixation in early childhood; an attachment to his mother which is then transferred to his father, in an attempt to conced more successfully the child's initial hostility; an attachment so strong that he is forced to reject all subsequent emotional involvement with women.

In addition, Nathaniel's horror at the sight of dark cavities seems to point to a displacement of the fear of castration from the father to the mother. It is a woman, Clara, who has death in her eyes.[36] Yet Nathaniel's well-being could only come from a woman, from his mother: it is his mother he finds at his bedside when he recovers from his fits of madness, and Clara whom he imagines saving him from the circle of fire in his poem. Because in the primal scene Nathaniel experienced a violent incestuous desire, subsequently he has castrated himself by renouncing women and identifying with a father fantasized as passive. Thus he has substituted narcissistic *jouissance* for the genital *jouissance* he has never had; the eyes for the genitals. Henceforth the partial instinct of sight plays the role of the genital instinct.

Voyeurism: the devil's eye

The fear of losing one's eyes is thus related to the fear of castration, but it is derived more directly from the lex talionis: it is related to a crime where the eyes are the source of guilt: 'if you have sinned with your eyes it is by your eyes that you will be punished'.[37]

Because Nathaniel is not the father, and also because he is

biologically immature, he can only have a representation, a forbidden representation, of sexual pleasure.[38] The importance of doubles in his subsequent life stems from this first substitution of the act by its representation: an originary representation that takes the place of an always forbidden presence. Nathaniel's eye has become diabolical because at a very early age it was diverted from its natural function and transformed into an organ of sexual pleasure. When an organ is symbolically diverted from its natural function it always ends up malfunctioning. The 'voyeur' in one way or another eventually loses his or her sight. In Nathaniel's case, this deficiency in the visual function is demonstrated by his inability to distinguish the animate from the inanimate, the real from the imaginary, and by the importance of his visions: Nathaniel always sees double, which explains the symbolic role played by spectacles and spy-glasses in the text. The latter, sold by Coppola, operate as veritable tempters: Nathaniel is seized by an irresistible urge to look and the devil takes possession of him every time he looks through his spy-glass. An insurmountable desire to look which forces him to lie in wait for the sandman and spy on him 'by some means or other':

> to investigate the mystery myself, to see the fabulous sandman myself – this desire grew more and more intense as the years passed. (p. 88)

> As my curiosity grew, so did my courage, and I would resolve to make the sandman's acquaintance by some means or other. Often I would creep out of my room into the corridor when my mother had gone past, but I could discover nothing, for the sandman would always be already inside the door by the time I had reached the place from which I might have seen him. At length, impelled by an irresistible urge, I decided to conceal myself within my father's room itself . . . in a moment I was in and behind the curtain drawn across an open cupboard. (ibid.)

> I had been discovered eavesdropping and mishandled by

> Coppelius. Fear and terror had brought on a violent fever with which I lay sick for many weeks. (p. 92)

An original crime which is responsible for his possession by the devil. 'Coppelius was in reality an evil force which had taken possession of him as he was hiding and listening behind the curtain' (p. 103). At the origin of all his other faults: his subsequent fate is marked by the repetition of the same compulsive act. He hides in order to spy on Olympia, who is herself hidden by a thick curtain and forbidden to the eyes of others (because, like Nathaniel's mother before her, she is kept a prisoner by the father): 'Recently I went upstairs in Professor Spalanzani's house and perceived that a curtain which was always drawn tight across a glass door up there was showing a chink of light. I don't know myself how I came to look through ... It made me feel quite uncanny, and I crept softly away into the neighbouring lecture room' (p. 98). 'He took up a small, very cleanly fashioned pocket-telescope and, in order to test it, looked out of the window. He had never in his life before handled a glass which brought objects to the eyes so sharply and clearly defined ... Involuntarily he looked into Spalanzani's room ... Nathaniel stood before the window as if rooted to the spot, lost in contemplation of Olympia's heavenly beauty' (p. 110).

The vision of a forbidden spectacle leaves him with a sense of guilt for which the reasons are displaced: 'Clara ... is surely right to consider me a tasteless spirit seer – yet it is odd – no, more than odd – that the foolish idea I might have bought the glass at too high a price still fills me with such strange trepidation. I can see no reason for it at all' (p. 111). It is the compulsive use of the spy-glass that makes him fall in love with an automaton and that is also at the root of his final crisis. Nathaniel himself attributes all his misfortunes to the diabolical spectacles. 'As soon as the spectacles had disappeared, Nathaniel became quite calm and, mindful of Clara, realised that the spectre which so terrified him could have proceeded only from his own mind, and that Coppola might be a highly honourable optician and mechanician but certainly not the revenant and doppelgänger of the accursed Coppelius' (p. 110).

Also, by way of negation, Nathaniel puts all his misfortunes down to his eyes: 'then you will be convinced that it is not the weakness of my eyes that renders the world colourless to me, but that a dark destiny really has suspended a veil of gloom over my life – a veil which I shall perhaps rend asunder only in death' (p. 92). The sandman who, having thrown sand in his eyes, blinds him for the rest of his days or makes him see double; a deficiency or over-exercise of the function that comes down to the same thing: a displacement of the procreative function from the genitals to the eyes which makes him engender doubles. Doubles which give him a perverse pleasure: the imitation of life replaces life.

The figures of the devil

Mimesis is here an originary mimesis because sexual pleasure as the mother's presence has never been given: the mother, as the Olympia episode shows, only ever appears at a distance, she is only glimpsed secretly. Neither is his father a unified, whole figure with whom Nathaniel can identify. Nathaniel is also a prisoner of doubles because he himself is always already divided: narcissism is the only means he seems to have at his disposal to attain unity and secure an identity for himself. If other characters are the father's doubles, it is because the father is always already diabolical – always double, and because double, triple, quadruple. The 'father' is a call for supplementarity because he is never self-identical. The devil is the power of division which separates the father from himself and from his kin. The devil's metamorphoses are the echo of the father's transformations, the father's selves are never perceived to coincide. Nathaniel's father is *unheimlich* because he reveals a double image of himself; the image of a being full of vitality and presence, the image of a being who is rigid and immobile, distant from all those around him. He appears to be the latter whenever Coppelius arrives: Coppelius, the man who introduces division and difference into the heart of family life and intimacy:

> Except at lunchtime, we, my brothers and sisters an I, saw little of our father all day. Perhaps he was very busy. After supper ... all of us, our mother as well, went into our father's study and sat around a table. Our father smoked and drank a large glass of beer. Often he told us strange stories and became so excited over them that his pipe went out and I hd to relight it for him with a burning spill, which I found a great source of amusement. But often he handed us picture books, sat silent and motionless in his armchair and blew out thick clouds of smoke, so that we were all enveloped as if by a fog. On such evenings our mother became very gloomy, and the clock had hardly struck nine before she said: 'Now children, to bed, to bed! The sandman is coming'. (p. 86)

The sandman is above all an intruder who puts an end to the security of the family group, who disrupts the intimacy of the proper and the near: the figure of the Stranger, the Other who brings sorrow and suffering, who takes away pleasure because he takes away the father's presence. 'Mama, who is this sandman who always drives us away from Papa?' (ibid.).

There can be no doubt that separation from the father and the anxiety this causes recalls the earlier anxiety the child experiences on being deprived of its mother during sexual intercourse: in both cases there is the same curiosity, the same anxiety. Moreover, the father's transformations during the course of the family's evening gatherings echo the way the parents are transformed during the primal scene: transformations reproduced in the sorcery scene in which the father is perceived as taking on a devilish appearance: 'as my father bent down to the fire, he looked quite different! A dreadful convulsive pain seemed to have distorted his gentle, honest features into a repulsive devil mask' (p. 91).

These changes in the father's appearance give rise to

doubts about paternal identity: is he good? Is he bad? But also, is he active? Is he passive? Man or woman? A hesitation that is to prove fatal to Nathaniel's development, preventing him from adopting a masculine position and keeping him in a state of ambivalence. The schizoid fear of fragmentation is linked to the impossibility of identifying with a stable image, even if it is experienced as a punishment for a crime both past and present. In this case it seems that the hysterical and neurotic complex of castration conceals a more primitive form of psychosis.[39]

For Freud the doublings of the father figure stem from the son's ambivalence towards his father, giving birth simultaneously to the devil and the good lord: 'In the story of Nathaniel's childhood, the figures of his father and Coppelius represent the two opposites into which the father-imago is split by his ambivalence.'[40]

> The evil demon of the Christian faith – the Devil of the Middle Ages – was, according to Christian mythology, himself a fallen angel and of a godlike nature. It does not need much analytic perspicacity to guess that God and the Devil were originally identical – were a single figure which was later split into two figures with opposite attributes. In the earliest ages of religion God himself still possessed all the terrifying features which were afterwards combined to form a counterpart to him. We have here an example of the process, with which we are familiar, by which an idea that has a contradictory – an ambivalent – content becomes divided into two sharply contrasted opposites. The contradictions in the original nature of God are, however, a reflection of the ambivalence which governs the relation of the individual to his personal father . . . Thus the father, it seems, is the individual prototype of both God and the devil.[41]

There can be no doubt that Nathaniel feels ambivalent towards his father, and that his feelings have led to a division between good and bad imagos: he wants to preserve the image of a father who is initially good, and only subsequently corrupted by the devil. But the division between the two is not absolute, since the father is corruptible, since he can transform himself into his opposite, just as the processes of alchemy mean to transform inert matter into living beings. The aim of such a division is to prevent any mixture, to maintain purity. Nathaniel is characterized precisely by the fact that he finds it impossible to fix secure boundaries, by his confusion of the animate and the inanimate, man and woman. What causes him such anxiety is not so much the duality of the figures but their tendency to merge into one another: that the same can become other. The ambivalence that derives from the Oedipus complex is grafted onto an inability to tolerate the ambivalence which always already exists in the father. Once more it covers up a more originary division; it masks the fact that the other always separates the same from itself. This ambivalence could not be efficient if, in the real, it did not converge with an even more originary division which is its condition of possibility. What conditions the 'devil' as the bad father is the existence of a more originary diabolical principle, the principle of division, the negative principle which Freud calls the death instinct. And because the latter could never be self-identical, because it is always plural, always other and different from itself, the figures of the devil are necessarily multiple. Strictly speaking, sheer ambivalence alone could not account for the multiplication of evil figures. In *The Sandman*, there is no character that does not, to some degree or another, bear the mark of evil. The figure of Nathaniel's father is corrupted by Coppelius, Clara carries the image of death in her eyes, Nathaniel is, like his father, divided by the evil principle. The mother is eliminated right from the beginning: Nathaniel asks Lothario not to tell her anything. She is the only figure whose good image must be preserved, the only one who can redeem the hero and thus the only one untainted by evil. But she remains too insubstantial to save him from madness and death.

In fact, perhaps this quasi-silence concerning his mother indicates in the final analysis that she is the most dangerous character of all – because she is the most desired. As for all the others, they are the embodiments of evil and death: the sandman whose seed is sterile and deadly; the lawyer Coppelius, whose choice of profession is not coincidental: by means of the formal and hollow powers of rhetoric, he is also in the habit of throwing sand in people's eyes, of deceiving them with 'machines of persuasion';[42] Spalanzani, the maker of automata who hoodwinks people by pretending to be a professor; Coppola, dealer in barometers, spectacles, spy-glasses, instruments of doubling, devilish instruments, also a creator of automata. Each of the figures of the devil is itself double (at least), deceptive: the satanic power of division is also always a power of simulacrum; indeed it the latter's condition of possibility; it is the power of the double in all its forms, inseparable from death. All sandmen throwing sand in others' eyes, the different representatives of the devil are themselves caricatures of life: there is something creaky, grimacing, some mark of the deathly 'machine' which distorts the living about them all: sardonic laughter, ugly grins, hoarse voices lend them all an uncannily similar appearance.

Is not the uncanniness of the death instincts, for which the figures of the devil serve as metaphors, the supreme form of *Unheimlichkeit*, the condition of all effects of the same type? And does it not derive from a universal case of repression, a case that is the most resistant of all: the repression of the presence of death within, and at the origin of, life itself?[43]

Postscriptum

For Phillipe Lacoue-Labarthe

At this point I think can hear the devil's sardonic laughter. He is happy that in my turn I too have fallen into his traps and lures, by mistaking the inanimate for the living, like Zeuxnis' birds or Buttner's monkey. By carrying out an analysis that seeks only to complicate the Freudian schema, which remains faithful to it by replacing one ultimate signified with another, more universal one, I am continuing to confuse fictional and real people. Having subjected the work to my desire for intelligibility, I have then consumed it greedily, without leaving any remainder, proving my bad taste, indeed my animality. What place, if this is not an idealist assumption, does this laughter come from? Hegel's critique of the traditional concept of mimesis will be discernible here: imitation is dangerous because it creates an illusion, and encourages fools to think they can devour the work of art without realizing that its essential function is to mirror the spirit, a divine mimetological mimesis and, as such, to be respected and venerated from a distance.

In opposition to such an idealist gesture, which presupposes a clearcut distinction between the living and the dead, the animate and the inanimate, the fictional and the real, and which turns the work of art into a work of pure imagination, the Freudian practice of treating fictional characters as if they were real people seems, in strategic terms, highly salutary. By establishing an essential link between the work and desire, by scotching the opposition between the imaginary and the real, Freud deconstructs the sacred character of art. Hoffmann, for whom the function of literature is the blurring of all boundaries and margins, for whom the real is a double of the imaginary, in a certain sense, authorizes an analytic kind of reading – a reading in which he himself is implicated.

On the other hand, however, Freud, by making a thematic reading of the text, by extracting from it an ultimate signified, the castration complex, responsible for the effect produced, seems trapped within the 'traditional logic of the sign'. He turns the text into a paradigmatic illustration of a truth exterior and anterior to it. The text thus called to witness is reinscribed in the process of analytic truth.

In turn, by taking the Freudian reading to its limit, by substituting the death instincts for the castration complex, have I simply replaced one theme with another, or have I 'surmounted' this kind of reading?

If one accepts the theory of the death instincts, it perhaps becomes pointless to oppose castration and the death instincts, since the latter become the condition of the former which, consequently, cannot play the role of a theme or an ultimate signified. With the theory of the death instincts, the work can no longer be the secondary illustration of an originary model full of sense, because such a hypothesis scotches any identity and plenitude of meaning and turns the text into an originary double.[44] With the notion of the death instincts understood as a principle of general economy,[45] the distinction between the imaginary and the real is replaced by a problematics of a simulacrum without an originary model. A 'diabolical' literature is no longer a literature of illusion or deception: it mimics the double as illusion by giving rise to 'effects' of sense and themes, in a mood of simulacrum and derision; introducing within the text a structure of duplicity which does not allow itself to be reappropriated into, or mastered by, a problematics of truth or falsehood.

Thus, although Hoffmann on the one hand authorizes an analytic reading, on the other, through the endless series of doublings in the text (of the paternal figure, for example), by the proliferation of the double in all its forms, he prevents any treatment of the double as just a theme like any other and, more especially, any attempt to find an ultimate meaning behind the text in the castration complex. By multiplying the double, he not only complicates any reading of the text by interweaving and amassing themes, he also makes such thematic interweaving the very law itself of the text. Because Freud wanted to make *The Sandman* a paradigm for all instances in which *Unheimlichkeit* derives from the return of repressed infantile complexes, he has obliterated precisely everything that stems from the double and the death instincts. Everything takes place as if Freud could not bear the importance of his discovery concerning the death instincts and as if *The Uncanny* with its successive invalidations, its tortuous procedure, is a last effort to conceal 'the return of the repressed' which emerges in the theory: an effort which once again proves the unacceptable nature of the theory of the death instincts.

But why is this theory so difficult to accept, unless it is because, in one way or another, it is connected with the prohibition on incest?

On several occasions I have emphasized how the importance of the figure of the mother is occluded both by Hoffmann in his story and by Freud in his interpretation. In this case Freud, who is normally so attentive to processes of inversion, remains on the level of the manifest text of the story and, like the story, he emphasizes the figure of the father and his doubles, neglecting even those details which could set him on the track of another interpretation (for example, the maternal nature of the sandman, who tears out children's eyes *as food for his [own] little children*).[46]

If the whole story can be read as a screen-fantasy concealing the incestuous desire for the mother and the threat of death which results from this desire, one might ask whether Hoffmann's insistence on the father's uncanniness, on the theme of paternal double, is not, in fact, a diabolical artifice designed to mask a quite different uncanniness, that of *writing* itself, supremely *unheimlich* because it repeats in symbolic form the forbidden sexual act: 'As soon as writing, which entails making a liquid flow out of a tube onto a piece of white paper, assumes the significance of copulation, or as soon as walking becomes a symbolic substitution for treading upon the body of mother earth, both writing and walking are stopped, because they represent the performance of a forbidden sexual act.'[47] Thus the theme of the double would have, in relation to this other uncanniness, an atropaic function.[48]

As we can see from Nathaniel's poetic 'creation' in *The Sandman*, writing is a diabolical production, a substitute for the child Nathaniel–Hoffmann desired to have with his mother, an imaginary child created at a distance, narcissistically, through the eyes, by identification with the father and mother, a gift subsequently offered to the mother in the guise of a substitute penis. What seems to be unbearable and *unheimlich* is this identification with the mother and the death which she threatens; this internalization of the forbidden mother, who can be considered an analogon of the death instincts.

Indeed we might well ask whether, in his turn, Freud's insistence on the theme of castration in a text which essentially has to do with literature (the specificity of which, as fiction, that is, as a production which is no longer simply the illustration of pre-existing themes, he is finally forced to recognize), whether his foregrounding of the theme, is not a way for him to master the text. That is, to master the incestuous and deadly function of writing: the simultaneous mastery of the text and the death instinct. Due, perhaps, to his own desire to write, his own desire to commit incest.

If the functioning of an organ is impaired when its sexual signification increases, if 'it behaves, if I may be allowed a rather absurd analogy, like a maid servant who refuses to go on cooking because her master has started an affair with her',[49] there is perhaps, for every writer, one vital defence: to travesty his text, to cover it over, to protect it behind a bundle of themes; or to ask endless questions about the 'fabrication of the text', which can also be a means of trying to master it.

Notes

Notes

On the Analytic Novel

Translator's note (hereafter given as 'TN'): unless indicated otherwise, all references to Freud are to the standard edition of his collected works, translated under the general editorship of J. Strachey (Hogarth 1953–66). The abbreviation SE has been used. Where Freud's *Gesammelte Werke* have been quoted, the abbreviation GW has been used. All quotations, unless indicated otherwise, are S. Kofman's.

1 These essays have all been published in the form of articles over the past five years: 'Freud and Empedocles' appeared in *Critique* (June 1969); 'Judith' in *Litterature* (October 1971); 'Summarize, interpret (*Gradiva*)' in *Critique* (October 1972); and 'The double is/and the devil' in *Revue Française de Psychanalyse* (January 1974). They have all been revised for this edition. [TN This Galilée edition appeared in 1974.]

2 Freud includes this novel in a list of ten favourite works in response to a questionnaire on reading in 1907 [SE, 9, p. 246]

3 Freud himself first gave *Moses and Monotheism* the title *Moses the Man, A Historical Novel.* Cf. his correspondence with A. Zweig, letter of 30 September 1934 [*The Letters of Sigmund Freud and Arnald Zweig*, ed. E.L. Freud, trans. Professor and Mrs W.D. Robson-Scott (Hogarth and Institute of Psycho-Analysis 1970)].

4 Cf. *Constructions in Analysis*, [SE, 23].

5 Cf. *L'Enfance de L'Art*, chapter 1 [S. Kofman, (Payot 1970, third edition Galilée 1985, translated as *The Childhood of Art*, Columbia University Press 1988)].

6 'Why disgrace Moses by putting my name to it? It is a joke but perhaps not a bad one' (Letter to Jones, 16 January 1914, quoted in *Life and Work of Sigmund Freud*, ed. E. Jones, complete edition (Hogarth 1955), p. 410). 'The Moses is anonymous partly as a pleasantry, partly out of shame at the obvious amateurishness which it is hard to avoid in papers for *Imago* and finally because my doubts about the findings are stronger than usual and I only published as a result of editorial pressure' (Letter to Abraham, 6 April 1914) [in *A Psychoanalytic Dialogue: The Letters of S. Freud and K. Abraham 1907–26*, ed. H.C. Abraham and E.L. Freud, trans. B. Marsh and H.C. Abraham (Hogarth 1965), p. 171]. He also says in a letter to his wife that *Moses* is a 'non-analytic' child. [TN Kofman gives no reference, but I found this expression in a letter of 12 April 1933 to Weiss, Freud's Italian translator, quoted in Jones, *Life and Work of Sigmund Freud*, vol. II, p. 411.]

7 Freud compares the analytic construction to 'a bait of falsehood taking a carp of truth'. Cf. *Constructions in Analysis*, SE, 23, p. 262.

8 TN The French here is *'être "relevé"'* *La relève* is Derrida's translation of the Hegelian concept of *Aufhebung*. Cf. Alan Bass's explanation in his translation of Derrida's 'La Différance' in *Les Marges de la Philosophie*: '*Aufhebung* literally means "lifting up", but it also contains the double meaning of conservation and negation. For Hegel, dialectics is a process of *Aufhebung*, every concept is to be negated and lifted up to a higher sphere in which it is thereby conserved ... *Aufheben*: Lift up, conserve, negate ... Derrida's translation is *la 'relève'*. The word comes from the verb *relever* which means to life up, as does *aufheben*. But *relever* also means to relay, to relieve, as when one soldier on duty relieves another. Thus the conserving-and-negating lift has become *la relève*, a "lift" in which is inscribed an effect of substitution and difference, the effect of substitution and difference inscribed in the double meaning of *Aufhebung*' (note 23, p. 19, of 'Différance', in *Margins of Philosophy*, trans. A. Bass (Hanover Press 1982)). See the rest of this quotation for a discussion of how the critique of *Aufhebung* fits into Derrida's general critique of metaphysics and his notion of *différance*. The usual English translation of '*Aufhebung*' is 'sublation', but I have decided to use the French '*relève*' untranslated where it occurs in this sense.

9 'When the child has grown up and has ceased to play, and after he has been labouring for decades to envisage the realities of life with proper seriousness, he may one day find himself in a mental situation which once more undoes the contrast between play and reality. As an adult he can look back on the intense seriousness with which he once carried on his games in childhood and by equating his ostensibly serious occupations of today with his childhood game he can throw off the too heavy burden imposed on him by life and win the high yield of pleasure afforded by humour.' Cf. *Creative Writers and Day-dreaming*, SE, 9, pp. 144–5.

10 *The Moses of Michaelangelo*, SE, 13, p. 211.

11 Family Romances, SE, 9, p. 240.

12 In this first work on Freud, for polemical reasons I placed a greater emphasis on the deconstructive aspect of Freud's writings. Certain very biased interpretations had been all too ready to classify him among the 'petit-bourgeois' metaphysicians. The present reading does not contradict the first, but stresses to a greater extent the heterogeneous character of Freudian texts.

13 TN Cf. Nietzsche, *Letze Arbeiten aus den Jahre 1875*. 'If only one could rediscover "these possibilities for life"! Poets and historians should brood upon this task; for such men are too rare to be allowed to slip through our fingers. One should, rather, give oneself no rest until one has reconstructed their pictures and painted them a hundred times on the wall [*hundertfach an die Wand gemalt*]' 'Das Philosophenbuch' (1872/3 and 1875) in *Gesammelte Werke*, ed. C.G. Naumann (Leipzig 1903), vol. X, p. 235. My translation.

14 For example, his study of Empedocles consists of a collection of quotations from Aristotle, first and final referant, all of whose conclusions Hegel fully endorses. Cf. Hegel, *Introduction*, p. 134.

15 TN My translation from 'Gedrucktes und Ungedrucktes aus den Jahren 1866–1877', *Gesammelte Werke*, 17, p. 352.

16 TN All references to Aristotle are taken from the revised Oxford translation of *The Complete Works of Aristotle*, ed. J. Barnes (Princeton UP 1984). Where the English translation differs from the French, this is indicated by a TN.

17 *Poetics*, 1459a. Cf. also *Rhetoric*, III, chapter 2. For the status of metaphor in Aristotelian philosophy see J. Derrida, 'La mythologie blanche', in *Marges de la Philosophie*, pp. 274ff. [TN

'White mythology', in *Margins of Philosophy*, trans. Bass, especially pp. 270ff.]

18 Cf. Derrida, 'La mythologie blanche', p. 294 [TN *Margins of Philosophy*, trans. Bass, p. 247]. Derrida distinguishes between **κυριὸν** and ἴδιον on the same page.

19 TN '*Avoir droit à la parole*'. The senses of having the authority to speak and of possessing the word – i.e. the truth – overlap here.

20 TN The French translation is '*balbutier*' and the English 'lisps'. I have used 'stammers'.

21 Cf. *Politics*, 1259b, 1277b, 1260a.

22 In one sense, in a temporal sense, actuality is prior to potentiality but in another it is not: '[T]he matter and the seed and that which is capable of seeing, which are potentially a man and corn and seeing, but not yet actually so, are prior in time to this particular man who now exists actually, and to the corn and to the seeing subject; but they are posterior in time to other actually existing things, from which they were produced. For from the potential, the actual is always produced from an actual thing' (*Metaphysics*, Book θ, 8, 1049b) [*Complete Works*, p. 1657]

23 TN '*Le propre de l'homme*', condensing the sense of property and propriety.

24 TN '*Le sens vrai s'éclaire lui-même*'.

25 TN '*Pensée qui se pense elle-même*'.

26 'From both these schools, then, we can learn this much, that the contraries are the principles of things; and how many these principles are and which they are, we can learn from one of these two schools. But how these principles can be brought together under the causes has not been clearly and articulately stated (σαφῶς μὲν οὐ διήρθρω ται) by them' (*Complete Works*, ed. Barnes, p. 1560).

27 TN The French for 'to have some inkling' is '*avoir comme pressenti*' and Kofman draws attention to the physical sense of the Greek: *touché/tâté/senti – pressenti*. What the English translates as 'vaguely' the French translates as '*obscurement*', stressing the Aristotelian metaphor of light and darkness for knowledge and ignorance.

28 TN '*La contribution des lumières de chacun*' – in the French the associations with light are more evident than in the English.

29 *Nichomachean Ethics*, I, 7, 1098.

30 Ibid., II, 1.
31 TN Cf. note 8 above.
32 Cf. J. Derrida, *Marges de la Philosophie*, p. 301 ['The Flowers of Rhetoric' in *Margins of Philosophy*, trans. Bass, p. 252].

Freud and Empedocles

1 Empedocles proved equally fascinating to Hölderlin, and particularly to Nietzsche. The latter ranked Empedocles, along with Goethe and Spinoza [and Heraclitus], among his precursors. Cf. Nietzsche, *Gesammelte Werke*, 14, p. 263, and 10 [ed. C.G. Naumann (Leipzig 1903)].
2 TN Schopenhauer, *The World as Will and Representation*, trans. E.F.J. Payne (Dover 1969), vol. I, p. 147.
3 TN I have used the translation of Empedocles' fragments by M.R. Wright (Yale UP 1981). He translates Empedocles' dual universal principles as 'love' and 'strife', but I have followed the French and translated them as 'love' and 'hate' ('*l'amour et l'haine*'). Where Kofman uses '*la discorde*' I have used 'strife'.
4 *Beyond the Pleasure Principle*, SE, 18, p. 7.
5 *An Autobiographical Study*, SE, 20, pp. 59–60.
6 Here again Nietzsche's ideas resemble Freud's. Nietzsche related, genealogically, any speculative assertion to an instinctive appraisal.
7 *The Psychopathology of Everyday Life*, SE, 6, pp. 258 and 259.
8 TN According to Wright, the fragments comprise 16–20 per cent of the total (*Empedocles*, p. 21). Cf. note 20 below.
9 Nietzsche in *Die Vorplatonischen Philosophen* also stresses the ambiguous nature of Empedocles' personality. 'If one traces all movement back to the action of incomprehensible forces, to attraction and repulsion, then the foundations of science dissolve into magic. Empedocles, however, remains continually poised on this borderline, and in almost all things he is just such a borderline figure. He hovers between doctor and magician, poet and rhetorician, god and human being, man of science and artist, statesman and priest, Pythagoras and Democritus. He is the most colourful figure in ancient philosophy: with him the age of myth, of tragedy, of orgy comes to a close, but equally the new Greek, the democrat, the orator, the rationalist, the allegorist, the man of science appears in him. Two ages contend within him: he is agonal man through and through' (Nietzsche,

'Die Vorplatonischen Philosophen', in *Gesammelte Werke*, vol. 19, p. 201. [TN My translation.]

10 *The Ego and the Id*, SE, 19, p. 46.

11 *Beyond the Pleasure Principle*, SE, 18, p. 49.

12 *Die Verneinung*, trans. as *Negation*, SE, 19, p. 235 and especially p. 237. Negation is the only thing that makes one recognize reality as such: it is only through a sense of absence or lack that the reality of presence can be felt: the moment of the 'no' in reality–testing is in the interval between 'finding' and 'refinding'.

13 Cited as proof of this hypothesis are the phenomena of fish migration and the phenomena of embryology [*New Introductory Lectures*, SE, 22, p. 106].

14 Freud refers to the phenomena of magnetic attraction and repulsion [ibid.].

15 '*Was nun folgt ist Spekulation, oft weitausholende Spekulation*' (GW, p. 23).

16 It is worth noting that the conceptions about sexuality in the myth of the *Symposium* and that of Empedocles are far from identical; they are even, in a certain sense, opposed. In the *Symposium*, there is the notion of an originary bisexuality, now lost, which strives for reconstitution. In Empedocles, androgyny is not the dream of a lost age but is created by the union of man and woman, which thus helps to bring about the restoration of the originary unity of the sphere. This unity is ontological and not sexual. The notion of bisexuality is, however, also to be found in Empedocles, on the level of the seed: sexual differentiation occurs as a function of the temperature of the uterus.

17 *Beyond the Pleasure Principle*, SE, 18, p. 59.

18 *New Introductory Lectures*, SE, 22, p. 95.

19 'Mit etwas Aufwand von Spekulation' (GW, 16, p.22; text addressed to Einstein) [SE, 22, p. 221].

20 A preliminary difficulty lies in the fragmentary nature of Empedocles' texts, which are known principally by doxography. Any reading of Empedocles therefore necessarily implies a reconstruction and an interpretation. Freud, as he says in *Analysis Terminable and Interminable*, knew Empedocles' writings only indirectly through Capella's book *The Presocratics*. My interpretation of certain texts follows Bollack's and will therefore not always conform to the traditional version of the texts famil-

iar to Freud. Thanks to the remarkable work of J. Bollack (*Empédocle* (Minuit 1965)) we now have a new and original understanding of Empedoclean thought. My reading follows Bollack's interpretation closely but I take full responsibility for the parallels drawn with Freud.

TN Wright's translation of Empedocles differs from the translation used by Kofman (trans. Jean Brun (Seghers 1966)) in its ordering of the fragments, in style and sometimes in interpretation, and it also differs from Bollack in some areas of interpretation. Wright says that 'the unsatisfactory state of the evidence for dividing and allocating the fragments that the original [Diels-Kranz] schema of groupings reveals has served as a check on any dogmatic conclusions derived from the original lines.' I have kept to the order of the fragments in the French translation to preserve the sense of the argument, but the numbers in parentheses after the English versions refer to Wright's translation. In case of any discrepancies I have decided to include the French version in full in TN. Any reader interested in finding out more about Wright's interpretation should refer directly to his work, particularly to the introduction and the commentary in part two. He also includes a useful concordance of the ordering of the fragments on p. 87.

21 [TN *Là on ne voit plus les membres agiles du soleil,*
Ni la puissance velue de la terre, ni la mer,
Tellement est fixé, dans l'épaisse enveloppe de l'Harmonie
Le Sphairos circulaire, joyeux dans sa révolution solitaire
Il n'y a ni discorde, ni lutte indécente dans ses membres.
Mais lui est égal en tous sens, semblable à lui-même et absolument sans limites.
Circulaire Sphairos, joyeux dans sa révolution solitaire
Car on ne voit pas deux branches s'élancer à partir de son dos
Il n'a pas de pieds, pas de genoux agiles, pas d'organes génitaux
Mais il est sphérique, en tous sens égal à lui-même.
(27, 28, 29)]

Cf. also fragments 13, 14, 132, 134 [10, 97 of Wright].

22 According to the Freudian view it is, on the contrary, the *Katharmoi* which would contain the truth of the *Physics*.

23 For the whole of this passage cf. fragments 112, 115, 117, 121, 122, 123, 125, 126, 130, 136, 137, and especially 117, 121,

and 137 [TN 102, 107, 108, 113, 116, 117, 130, 110, 118, 119, 122, 124 of Wright].

In particular 108: 'For before now I have been at the same time boy and girl / Bush, bird, and a mute fish in the sea' ['*Car moi j'ai déjà été un garçon, une fille / Une plante, un oiseau et un poisson muet qui bondit audessus de la mer*'].

121: 'A joyless place / Where there is slaughter and hatred and hordes of other violent deaths / And parching fevers and consumptions and dropsy / They wander in Darkness on the field of Ate' ['*Terre sans joie / Où la mort et la Haine et les autres Génies de la Mort / Et les maladies qui ravagent et les putréfactions et les oeuvres de la dissolution / Errent sur la prairie du malheur dans les Ténèbres*'].

137: 'The father will lift up his dear son in a changed form, / And blind fool, as he prays will slay him / And those who take part in the sacrifice bring the victim as he pleads / But the father, deaf to his cries, slays him in his house and prepares an evil feast. / In the same way son seizes father and children their mother, / And having bereaved them of life devour the flesh of those they love' ['*Le père ayant soulevé son fils qui a changé de forme, / Le tue en priant, l'insensé! mais ils implorent la pitié / Et se précipitant vers les meurtriers, alors que lui, de son côté, sourd aux cris des victimes, le tue / Le tue, préparant dans sa demeure le festin infâme. / De même le fils saisit son père, les enfants leur mère, / Et leur arrachant la vie, ils dévorent la chair de leurs propres parents*'].

24 In this he differs from, for example, Anaxagoras, who regards the *noûs* as the only principle.

25 Cf. Nietzsche, *Das Philosophenbuch*, Historiche Darstellung, II, p. 96, in *Gesammelte Werke*, 10 ['Die Symbolik des Geschlechtsliebe']

26 Cf. Dr Green's articles in *L'Inconscient*, nos 1 and 2. He gave an initial version of this work in his seminar in 1968 at the Institut de Psychanalyse. My thanks to A. Green. [TN My translation.]

27 TN *Analysis Terminable and Interminable*, SE, 23, p. 246.

28 That is: Philotes and Philia = friendship, Aphrodite = the goddess of love, Kypris = the goddess of desire, Storgê = tenderness.

29 That is: strife (a term from the Iliad), war, conflict, division.

30 I am following Bollack's interpretation very closely here.

31 [TN '*Double ce que je dirais: tantôt l'Un s'accroît pour seul être de*

plusieurs qu'il était, tantôt au contraire il se sépare pour être plusieurs, d'Un qu'il fut.']

The double interpretation it is possible to make of Empedoclean cosmogony is reminiscent of the opposing genetic (theory of stages) and structural (theory of a cycle) interpretations of Freud. In the latter case, both interpretations must be accepted as valid.

32 The other functions of the death instinct which I mentioned previously do not appear in Empedocles.

33 TN SE, 19, p. 164.

34 TN SE, 23, p. 149.

35 TN SE, 19, p. 42.

36 TN '*Point de naissance pour aucune chose mortelle,/ Point de fin dans la Mort funeste*' (8).

37 TN No reference given. According to Wright's arrangement, this is a combination of fragment 60 with part of fragment 47:

De l'eau, de la terre, de l'éther et du soleil
Mêlés, sont nées les formes et les couleurs des choses mortelles
Qui toutes vivent maintenant accordées par les soins d'Aphrodite,
Et comme elles se mélangeaient voici que se répandaient
Les Myriades de tribus mortelles
Ajustées à des formes diverses, merveilles à voir.

38 TN No reference given.

Un lien les unit tous dans toutes leurs parties
Splendeur solaire, et terre, ciel et mer
Qui loin d'eux, dans les choses mortelles vivent égarés
Et de même toutes celles qui davantage répugnent au mélange
S'aiment l'une l'autre appareillées par Aphrodite.
Mais les plus ennemies s'éloignent l'une de l'autre au plus loin
Dans leur race, dans le mélange et dans les figures façonnées
Etrangères à toute étreinte, devenues maléfiques
Sur les conseils de Discorde.

39 Aristotle and Nietzsche both emphasize this point when discussing Empedocles. 'In [the story of] living beings Empedocles also . . . denies purpose [*Zweckmässigkeit*]. It is his greatest feat.' Cf. Nietzsche, *Das Philosophenbuch*, II, *Gesammelte Werke*, 10, p. 96. [TN My translation.]

40 '*Elle est Nécessité, apanage de dieux, antique loi, / Loi éternelle que*

cerclent de larges sceaux.' [TN 'There is a degree of necessity, ratified long ago by the gods, eternal and sealed by broad oaths' (107).]

41 TN No reference given.

> *En foule croissaient, doubles par la face et le torse*
> *Des espèces bovines à troncs d'hommes. D'autres surgissaient*
> *Sorte d'hommes à tête de boeuf, mixtes, tenant là du mâle*
> *Et là, ce sont des femelles aux membres d'ombres.*

42 This was one of Freud's arguments in favour of the compulsion to repeat in *Beyond the Pleasure Principle*; cf. SE, 18, p. 44.

43 TN No reference given.
'*En foule, la terre fit germer des tempes sans nuque / Des bras rôdaient, nus, veufs d'épaule / Et des yeux erraient, solitaires, frustrés de front.*'

44 Thus there can already be found in Empedocles the notion that there are other kinds of sexuality apart from genital sexuality. In particular, his idea that the eye was an erogenous zone was bound to interest Freud.

45 TN No reference given. For Nietzsche on Socrates, see, 'Vom Denken beherrschtes heben' (cf. *Gesammelte Werke*, 9, p. 65). Also cf. ibid., 19, *Die Vorplatonischen Philosophen*, pp. 224ff, and 10, *Wissenschaft und Weisheit im Kampft*, pp. 216–37.

46 Cf. Nietzsche, *Theoretische Studien* 1872/3, 1875, *Gesammelte Werke*, pp. 125–6.

47 TN Cf. the chapter '*On the analytic novel*', note 8.

Judith

1 Freud, GW, 12, pp.161 ff; SE, 10, pp. 193 ff.

2 Cf. *Constructions in Analysis*, GW, 16, p. 44; SE, 23, p. 258. 'What sort of material does he put at our disposal which we can make use of to put him on the way to recovering lost memories? All kinds of things ... It is out of such raw material ... that we have to put together what we are in search of.'

3 Cf. *New Introductory Lectures: Revisions in Dream Theory*, GW, 15; SE, 22, pp. 23–4.

4 'The forms assumed by the different neuroses echoed the most highly admired productions of our culture' (Reik's *Preface to Ritual: Psychoanalytical Studies*, GW, 12; SE, 17, p. 261).

5 Cf. *Preface to Totem and Taboo* and *On the Teaching of Psychoanalysis in Universities*, SE, 17, p. 173.

6 'The neuroses exhibit on the one hand striking and far-reaching points of agreement with those great social institutions art, religion, and philosophy. But on the other hand they seem like distortions of them' (*Totem and Taboo*, SE, 13, p. 73).

7 In *The Moses of Michaelangelo* Freud calls himself a 'layman', and also in *The Uncanny*, in which he uses the same method.

8 Cf. Klee's parable of the tree in *On Modern Art*: 'This sense of direction in nature and life, this branching and spreading array, I shall compare with the root of the tree . . . Thus he [the artist] stands as the trunk of the tree . . . I have already spoken of the relationship between the root and the crown, between nature and art; and have explained it by a comparison of earth and air, and with the corresponding different functions of below and above. The creation of a work of art . . . must of necessity, as a result of entering into the specific dimensions of pictorial art, be accomplished by a distortion of the natural form.' [TN Trans. P. Findlay, (Faber and Faber 1948), pp. 13–19.]

9 Cf. *The Interpretation of Dreams* and *Totem and Taboo*.

10 This conception of female sexuality is inscribed in a whole tradition fathered by Aristotle. For the latter everything becomes what it is when it reaches its complete state of development. There are as many 'natures' as there are degrees of perfection of the substantial form of the essence. The 'right to speech/the word' ['*à la parole*'; cf. the chapter 'On the Analytic Novel', note 19] and therefore to the phallus is also a function of the degree of perfection of the essence. Cf. 'Aristotle and the presocratics' above.

11 *Analysis Terminable and Interminable*, GW, 16; SE, 23, p. 252.

12 In numerous texts, Freud stresses the superiority of poetic knowledge over scientific knowledge. Cf. *L'Enfance de L'Art* [S. Kofman (Payot 1970); translated as *The Childhood of Art*, Columbia University Press 1988].

13 *The Psychopathology of Everyday Life*, SE, 6, p. 258, note 2.

14 *The Taboo of Virginity*, p. 266.

15 Cf. 'The Double is/and the Devil' below, pp. 119ff.

16 It did not escape the attention of Spinoza that one of the reasons for the corruption of the biblical text was sexual repression. This is how he later explains the difference between the text and the marginal notes. Thus the term for a 'young girl' is

always, except in one passage, spelt without the letter *he* in the text, while in the marginal notes it is written correctly according to the grammatical rules. The marginal notes would thus not all be 'various readings' of 'obscure and doubtful doctrinal passages', but would 'mark expressions which have passed out of common use, obsolete words and terms which current decency did not allow in a public assembly.' [TN Cf. p. 143 of the *Tractus Theologico-Politicus*, trans. R.H.M. Elwes, (Dover 1951).]

'The ancient writers, without any evil intention employed no comely paraphrase, but called things by their plain names. Afterwards, through the spread of evil words and luxury, words which could be used by the Ancients without offence come to be considered obscene. There was no need for this cause to change the text of Scripture. Still, as a concession to popular weakness, it became the custom to substitute more decent terms for words denoting sexual intercourse, excreta sic., and to read them as they were given in the margin' (ibid., pp. 141 and 142).

Originally, the text made no gender distinction: 'young person' was the only term used. Likewise, there was a single pronoun: 'him' or 'her' self was not differentiated. It seems that the process of repression goes hand in hand with an accentuation of sexual difference. Does this mean that originary bisexuality is increasingly repressed because of an increased fear of castration?

17 Freud establishes the same relation between the clarity of psychoanalysis and the obscurity of poetic knowledge as Aristotle does between philosophy and myth. Both approach myths and symbols in a ritualistic, reductive fashion. Myth is said to contain potentially and in an indeterminate state the truth which only philosophy actualizes. Cf. Aristotle, *Metaphysics*, A, 982, and above, pp. 9–19.

18 *The Taboo of Virginity* [p. 198].

19 *F. Hebbel, Ein Psychoanalytischer Versuch* (Nendelm/Liechtenstein 1920).

20 Cf. *Dostoievsky and Parricide* [SE, 21] in which Freud repeats the same idea in regard to S. Zweig's statements about *Four and Twenty Hours in A Woman's Life*. [TN 'It is interesting to notice how the façade given to the story by its author seeks to disguise its analytic meaning' (SE, 21, p. 193).]

21 TN My translation.
22 Quoted by Sadger. [TN My translation from p. 322, *F. Hebbel.*]
23 Letter, 14 January 1843, quoted by Sadger. [TN P. 323, of *F. Hebbel.*]
24 Quoted by Sadger. [TN My translation from a letter to Ruge, 15 February 1852, p. 321, *F. Hebbel.*]
25 *Moses and Monotheism*, GW, 15; SE, 23, p. 85.
26 'Kindly Nature has given the artist the ability to express his most secret mental impulses, which are hidden even from himself, by means of the works he creates, and these works have a powerful effect on others who are strangers to the artist, and who are themselves unaware of the source of their emotion' (*Leonardo da Vinci and a Childhood Memory*, GW, 8; SE, 11, p. 107).
27 TN All references are to the C. van Doren translation of Hebbel's *Judith and Holofernes* (R.G. Badger 1912). I have on occasion modified this translation.
28 Cf. Freud, *New Introductory Lectures: Revision of Dream Theory* [SE, 22, p. 24].
29 Cf. Schreber, who elaborates a whole system of delusions allowing him to reconcile his belief in God with enjoyment of forbidden homosexual pleasure [SE, 12, p. 48]. See also *Gradiva*, in which scientific motives for Norbert's behaviour cover up an erotic motive: 'It should not be forgotten, however, that the unconscious determination could not effect anything that did not simultaneously satisfy the conscious scientific ones' [TN Jensen's *Gradiva*, SE, 9, p. 52].
30 Cf. a similar attitude in one of Julien Green's heroines in *Si J'Étais Vous* (Plon 1947), pp. 249–59.
31 Cf. Freud, 'Posthumous fragments', in *L'Arc*, issue dedicated to Freud.
32 Freud, *The Theme of The Three Caskets*, SE, 12, p. 301.
33 Cf. G. Roheim, *Australian Totemism: A Psychoanalytic Study In Anthropology*, trans. M.D. Eder (Allen and Unwin 1925).
34 'A person may love: (1) According to the narcissistic type (a) What he himself is (i.e. himself) (b) What he himself was (c) What he himself would like to be (d) Someone who was once part of himself. (2) According to the anaclitic (attachment) type: (a) The woman who feeds him (b) The man who protects him' (*On Narcissism: An Introduction*, SE, 14, p. 90).

35 Generally, here as elsewhere, Freud gives only a vague 'summary' of the text he is using. I will therefore carry out my own 'supplementary' analysis of the text, which means that there will be certain displacements in relation to Freud's own interpretation.

36 This fantasy of theft is reminiscent of Artaud's desire to be his own progenitors: he calls God 'the great thief'. Cf. J. Derrida, 'La parole souffle' in *L'Ecriture et La Différance* (Seuil 1967) [TN trans. A. Bass, in *Writing and Difference* (Routledge and Kegan Paul 1978)]. Cf. also the film *The Conversation*, where the anxiety of the person who eavesdrops on secret conversations, his fear of being spied on in turn, can be traced back to the primitive anxiety stemming from the destruction of bodily integrity, against which he defends himself by his narcissism.

37 In the sense used by Ferenczi in 'Introjektion und Ubertragung' [TN trans. E. Jones, as 'Introjection and transference', in *First Contributions to Psychoanalysis* (Hogarth 1952), pp. 47 and 48].

38 'It would be hard to say whether and when we have succeeded in mastering this factor in an analytic treatment. We can only console ourselves with the certainty that we have given the person analysed every possible encouragement to re-examine and alter his attitude to it' (*Analysis Terminable and Interminable*, SE, 23, pp. 252 and 253). 'The writer ... [enables] us to thenceforward ... enjoy our own daydreams without self-reproach or shame' (*Creative Writers and Day-Dreaming*, SE, 9, p. 53). Thus for Freud, it is in aesthetic pleasure that the three psychic agencies are reconciled: each agency finds satisfaction in aesthetic pleasure: as in Kant, aesthetic pleasure is proof of the harmony of human faculties.

Summarize, Interpret (*Gradiva*)

1 TN My translation of the following: '*Ou bien ... il faut que je m'interdise tout raccourci, c'est-à-dire tout choix, ou bien je leur suis infidèle ... et je me hasarderais à quelque choix, à quelque raccourci. Mais alors, dans cette deuxième hypothèse, au premier soupçon d'infidélité, au premier symptôme, je ne suis plus moi-même selon eux; au premier symptôme, c'est un procédé d'art, une méthode d'art et aussitôt je suis encore perdue. Vous ne me tirerez pas de ce dilemme: ou bien, je suis sotte, ou bien je suis infidèle; ou bien, je veux comme ils*

veulent, épuiser l'indéfinité du détail, et alors je ne peux jamais pas même commencer mon commencement. Ou bien, je lâche, fût-ce d'un atome, la totale indéfinité du détail et alors d'autre part, je perds tout, car tout mon prétendu système de sécurité tombe.'

2 TN Freud, *Delusions and Dreams in Jensen's Gradiva* (1907), SE, 9, pp. 3–94. All references to Jensen's text are to the translation by H.M. Downey in *Delusion and Dream: An Interpretation in the Light of Psychoanalysis of Gradiva* (Allen & Unwin 1921).

3 As for Norbert's second dream (cf. pp. 32 and 33 of Jensen), Freud omits it from the summary. This omission is perhaps due to the fact that it hardly affects the hero's behaviour. However, it could also be because it can hardly be used as proof of the validity of the psychoanalytic interpretation: it can be explained purely in terms of the day's events and by the use of symbols.

4 Freud does so constantly: his use of the 'summary' is widespread. Cf. the analysis carried out in *The Ratman*, where a similar operation is effected on the original text, *The Journal of the Ratman*, Freud's record of the daily consultations (itself probably 'a mutilated telegraph message').

5 TN My translation.

6 Satisfaction of the ego and the id, and also of the superego, since enjoyment takes place in ignorance of the 'suspect' sources of the pleasure.

7 'He [the author] wishes to bring the hero closer to us so as to make "empathy" easier; the diagnosis of "*degeneré*", whether it is right or wrong, at once puts the young archaeologist at a distance from us, for we readers are the normal people and the standard of humanity' (Freud, *Delusions and Dreams*, SE, 9, p. 45). 'He [the hero] still appears to us as incomprehensible and foolish; we have no idea how his peculiar folly will be linked to human feeling and so arouse our sympathy. It is an author's privilege to be allowed to leave us in such uncertainty. The charm of his language and the ingenuity of his ideas offer us a provisional reward for the reliance we place in him and the still unearned sympathy which we are ready to feel for his hero' (*Delusions and Dreams*, SE, 9, p. 14).

8 Cf. *Delusions and Dreams*, SE, 9, p. 44.

9 'We may suspect that . . . our case of illness might end up as a commonplace love story . . . and was not our hero's infatuation for his Gradiva sculpture a common instance of being in love,

though of being in love with something past and lifeless?' (Freud, *Delusions and Dreams*, SE, 9, p. 22).

10 This is not a disinterested pleasure: the desire for knowledge is also rooted in the libido. For the reader, the pleasure of solving a mystery is a substitute for the pleasure he gets from the extraordinary and magical elements [*le merveilleux*] or the fantastical nature of the story. A further disappointment lies in store – he discovers Zoe is only Norbert's neighbour: the mystery was too simple. Freud shows that what is magical [*merveilleux*] is the detailed apprehension of the links between the delusional creation and everyday reality. If the psychoanalyst deconstructs the fantastical, he reinstates it in a different form. The extraordinary and magical [*le merveilleux*] lies within us. (Cf. on this subject *The Uncanny* and Plato's *Phaedrus*, 230 a.)

11 In his essay, Freud continuously and implicitly draws a parallel between, on the one hand, dreams and delusions, and, on the other, fictional productions. The same terms are used to describe them: both seem at first to be arbitrary products of the imagination ('Such products of the imagination would seem to us astonishing and inexplicable if we met them in someone in real life. Since our hero . . . is a fictitious person, we perhaps put a timid question to his author, and ask whether his imagination was determined by forces other than its own arbitrary choice' (pp. 14–15)), but Freud interprets them as 'echoes', repetitions of the past, and as such subject to fixed psychic laws (cf. pp. 45 and 14). He uses the same metaphors to describe them: the metaphors of 'tissue' and of 'construction'.
[TN The metaphors of '*tissu*' and '*édifice*' which Kofman uses are translations from the original german '*Gespinst*' (and its derivatives '*Wahngespinst*' and '*Hirngespinst*': cf. GW, 7, pp. 53, 63, 97) and '*Bildung*' ('*Wahnbildung*') or '*Gebaude*' ('*Wahngebaude*': cf. ibid., pp. 33, 105, 106). Freud also employs the terms '*Gedanken-gewebe*' (p. 86) and '*Aufstelling*' (p. 115) respectively. He uses verbs with a metaphorical sense both of weaving of spinning (*verweben, ausgesponnen, umspann:* cf. pp. 99 and 39) and of building or constructing (*zurechtgearbeitet, zusammenschweisst*: cf. pp. 58, 103, 104). The SE uses both 'tissue' (p. 50) and 'cobweb' (pp. 33 and 37) for '*Gespinst*', and 'structure' (pp. 9 and 22) for '*Bildung*'. However, as the English does not always convey the same metaphorical sense as the original Ger-

man or the passages Kofman quotes from the French (Payot) translation, I feel it necessary to include here all three versions.]

1 For the metaphor of tissue/web:

Il est évidemment tout à fait guéri de son délire, il le domine, ce qu'il démontre en brisant lui-même les derniers fils de la toile. (p. 167)

Evidently he was completely cured of his delusion ... and he proved this by himself tearing the last threads of the cobweb of his delusion. (p. 37)

Er ist offenbar von seinem Wahn geheilt ... und beweist dies, indem er die letzten faden des Wahngespinstes Selbststandig zerreist. (p. 63)

Les malades atteignent à des records dans l'art de tisser en une trame cohérence des absurdités plausibles. (p. 214)

in severe cases of chronic delusions (in paranoia) the most extreme examples occur of ingeniously elaborated and well-supported absurdities. (p. 72)

in ersten fullen chronischer Wahnbilding (Paranoia) das Ausserste, an geistreich ausgesponnenen und gut vetretenen Absurditaten geleistet wird. (p. 99)

Le jeune homme qui vient de parler file en son cerveau une toile étrange, il me semble qu'il se figure qu'une mouche lui bourdonne dans la tête; d'ailleurs chacun n'a-t-il pas son araignée au plafond? [TN No reference given]

The young man who's just gone off is labouring, like you, under a remarkable aberration. He seems to think there's a fly buzzing in his head. Well, I expect everyone has some kind of insect there. (p. 27)

Der junger Herr, der ebeb fortging, laboriert auch an einem merkwirdigen Hirngespinst, mir scheint, er glaubt, dass ihn eine Gleige in Kopfe summt; non, irgend eine Kerbtierart hat wohl jeder drin. (p. 53)

2 For the metaphor of structure/construction:

Gradiva lui démontre l'inanité de tout cet edificé et lui fournit les explications les plus naturelles sur tout ce qui lui semblait énigmes. (p. 232)

Gradiva ... had shown him that all his hypotheses were incorrect and ... had given him the most natural explanations of everything puzzling. (p. 87)

Gradiva selbst ihn die Unrichtigheit all seiner Aufstellungen überfuhre und ihm die naturlichsten Erklarungen für alles Ratselhafte gebe. (p. 115)

Nouvelle pièce de la constuction délirante. (p. 222)

A curious new piece of delusion. (p. 78)

Dies ist doch ein Sonderbares Stuck neuer Wähnbilding. (p. 105)

Comprendre la genèse de ce complément au délire, rechercher quel nouveau fragment de l'inconscient se fait jour par substitution sans ce nouveau fragment de délire. [TN No reference given]

To explain the origin of this addition to the delusion and to look for the fresh piece of unconscious discovery which was replaced by the fresh piece of delusion. (p. 78)

die Entstehung dieses Wahnzuwachses verstandlich zu machen, das neue Stuck unbewusster Einsicht aufzusuchen, das sich durch das neve Stuck Wahn ersetzt. (p. 105)

Finally, dream, delusion and fictional production are *enigmatic* texts:

A group of men who regarded it as a settled fact that the essential riddles of dreaming have been solved by the author of the present work. (p. 7)

Once they [the patients] have understood, they themselves bring forward the solution of the final and most important riddles of their strange condition. (p. 38)

[H]er [Zoe's] ultimate translation of the delusion. (p. 88) [TN '*Zoé a resolu l'enigme du delire.*']

The author presents us with a further puzzle by making the dream, the discovery of the supposed Gradiva in the street and the decision to undertake the journey as a result of the singing canary succeed one another as a series of chance events without any internal connection with one another. (p. 66)

For a discussion of Freud's repeated use of such metaphors, cf. my *L'Enfance de L'Art*, particularly chapter 3 [trans. as *The Childhood of Art*].

12 Cf. J. Derrida, *La Dissemination*, pp. 264ff (Seuil 1972) [*Dissemination*, trans. B. Johnson (UC/Athlone Press 1981), pp. 64ff].

13 Cf. Particularly *The Ratman*, in which Freud makes great use of this method.

14 TN The French for 'melted into a unity' is '*s'identifient*': the 'technical term' introduced is that of identification.

15 Cf. *The Moses of Michaelangelo*, in which Morelli's method is used as a model.
16 TN '*L'espace de lisibilité de l'oeuvre*'.
17 Cf. *The Ratman*, SE, 10, p. 223.
18 Cf. Nietzsche [in the Preface to 'Philosophy during the Tragic Age of the Greeks', in *Collected Works*, ed. O. Levy, (J. N. Foulis 1909–13) vol. II, p. 74], who opposes the summaries of philosophers in textbooks, 'tedious' because they silence 'the personal element', to those summaries which, even though they give an incomplete picture of a philosopher's life, convey this personal element.
19 The spade is a reminder of the pitchfork from Horace's lines, quoted by Freud, '*Naturam furca expellas, tamen usque recurret*' (p. 35). A year later in *The Ratman*, Freud will use the symbolism of Pompeii on his own account (p. 176): 'I then made some short observations upon the psychological differences between the conscious and unconscious and upon the fact that . . . what was unconscious was relatively unchangeable, . . . the destruction of Pompeii was only beginning now that it had been dug up.'
20 'He possessed a certain skill in deciphering "graffiti" which were difficult and had already accomplished widely recognised work in that field' (p. 47 of Jensen).
21 In particular, (p. 35) '[H]e considered them [the common house fly] the basest evil intention of Nature, on their account much preferred the winter to the summer as the only time suited to human life and recognised in them invincible proof against the existence of a rational world system.' (p. 38) 'Thus under the glowing sun of the Campagna, there was a mythological-literary-historical-archaeological juggling in his head.' (p. 52) 'The sun stretched out a golden carpet on the old lava-blocks; Vesuvius spread its misty pine-cone; and the whole excavated city seemed overwhelmed, not with pumice and ashes, but with pearls and diamonds, by the beneficent rain storms. The brilliance in the eyes of the young daughter of the zoologist rivalled these.' (pp. 107 and 108).
22 The opposition between the Hotel Switzerland (where the '*bons vivants*' stay) and The Diomed (where those obsessed with dead antiquities stay) can be inserted into the same system. The intermediate place would be The Sun, the inn as yet unknown to Norbert.

23 *The Three Caskets* [SE, 12, p. 297].
24 Cf. *Infantile Genital Organisation*, SE, 19, pp. 144–5.
25 TN The French is '*Méduser*'.
26 Cf. pp. 26, 48, 62, 73 of Jensen.
27 Cf. *Medusa's Head*, SE, 18, pp. 273 and 274.
28 Cf. pp, 23 and 24 of *Gradiva*, where Norbert, seeing Gradiva walking, from a distance and from above, has difficulty in recognizing her with any certainty.
29 In *The Ratman*, Freud appears to attribute the formation of symptoms, and word plays, to chance. Thus, by chance, one should understand an apparent external contingency which reflects a psychic necessity: 'Chance may play a part in the formation of a symptom, just as the wording may help in the making of a joke' (p. 210).
30 Cf. *Jokes* [SE, 8, pp. 37ff].
31 Since this text was published, I have written on Freud's *Jokes* in *Pourquoi Rit-on* [S. Kofman] (Galilée 1986).
32 *Jokes*, p. 103.
33 Cf. *The Antithetical Meaning of Primal Words* [SE, 11]: primal words bear two opposed meanings. Cf. My *Un Philosophe Unheimlich* in *Ecarts*, p. 173 [S. Kofman (Fayard 1973)]. This text is also in my *Lectures de Derrida* [S. Kofman] (Galilée 1985). In this, I analyse the relation between the Freudian text and the Hegelian conception of speculative words with double meanings in German.
34 Cf. 'Le protocole de *L'Homme aux Rats*' in *Revue Française de Psychanalyse* (July 1971) and p. 21 of *Dream and Delusion*: 'It is only to us that the source of her remarks sound as though they had a double sense, as though besides their meaning in the context of the delusion they also meant something real and present day.'
35 The formation of compromises in which two opposing desires are able to find satisfaction at the same time is characteristic of the mental processes of hysterics: one phrase is often invented by the patient to express two opposing meanings: 'to kill two birds with one stone'. Cf. *The Ratman*, p. 192, note 1, and p. 196.
36 '[A] full view of her face . . . produced in him a double feeling, for it appeared to him at the same time unknown and yet also familiar, already seen or imagined' (p. 55 of Jensen).

37 'Assault and resistance are renewed after the construction of each compromise, which is never, so to speak, entirely satisfying. Our author is too aware of this and that is why he makes a peculiar unrest dominate this stage of his hero's disorder' (p. 52 of Freud).

38 'The creation of uncertainty is one of the methods employed by the neurosis for drawing the patient away from reality and isolating him from the world which is among the objects of every psychoneurotic disorder' (*The Ratman*, p. 232).

The Double is/and the Devil

1 In German this would be translated as '*Sand in die Augen streuen*'. [TN The French '*jeter de la poudre aux yeux*' conveys the metaphorical sense of blinding and the associations with the sandman on which Kofman plays.]

2 GW, XII, p. 229 [SE, 17, p. 219]. What follows is not a comprehensive analysis of *The Uncanny*, a reading I began in 'Un philosophe *Unheimlich*' in Lucette Finas, S. Kofman, Roger Laporte and Jean-Michel Rey, *Écarts: quatres essais à propos de Jacques Derrida* (Fayard 1973) and in S. Kofman, *Lectures de Derrida* (Galilée 1985). What I am using is simply an outline of the text, the schema (which would need to be 'complicated' and made more nuanced) that is necessary to ascertain the place of the sandman paradigm within the text.

3 We may well ask whether Freud's affirmation is not, in fact, a negation, since several pages later (p. 237) he recalls his feelings of uncanniness on finding himself three times in succession back in the red-light district of an Italian town – precisely the district he was trying to avoid.

4 Cf. pp. 211 and 212 [SE, 13].

5 Freud finds his precursor for this in Morelli: 'It seems to me that his method of inquiry is closely related to the technique of psychoanalysis. It too is accustomed to divine secret and concealed things from unnoticed features, from the rubbish heap as it were, of our own observations' (ibid., p. 222).

6 A diversity emphasized in particular by Jentsch. He is the only one, apart from being the only non-aesthetician, who pays any attention to the uncanny. But not, however, 'exhaustively' (p. 219).

7 At the very beginning, Freud alludes to the war which has prevented him from studying foreign literature in any depth (pp. 219–20). Also, in more general terms, the '*unheimlich*' character of the Freudian text (which is so wily and perverse that it concludes by according fiction a privileged character while at the same time, on the level of its analyses, it ignores the specificity of literature) leads one to conclude that a fundamental conflict is being played out within it.

8 TN '*En abîme*'.

9 TN The French '*demeurer en reste*' plays on the notion of the '*reste*': psychoanalysis does not want any fictional surplus to escape its schema of uncanny effects.

10 Fictional conventions permit the adult to be a child once more: for the duration of his or her reading, the adult is spared the effort of having to adapt to the real. The pleasure in magical and extraordinary events [*le merveilleux*] consists of this additional saving of psychic energy. [TN The position of this footnote is not marked on the original text.]

11 Cf. pp. 85ff above.

12 This novel is analysed by me in 'Vautour rouge', in *Mimesis des Articulations* [S. Kofman] (Flammarion 1975).

13 Cf. J. Derrida (nearly all his texts, but particularly *La Dissémination*, p. 50) and what I have to say on the subject in *Écarts*, pp. 188ff, and in *Lectures de Derrida*.

14 It is notable that Freud never refers to the fact that the sandman tears out children's eyes *in order to feed his own children*, thus concealing the 'maternal' nature of this apparently masculine figure.

15 Formalism is, moreover, simply the flip-side of thematism: both belong to the same system.

16 For the relationship between Coppelius and Coppola, Freud refers us to the following etymology: 'Frau Dr Rank has pointed out the association of the name with *Coppella* – crucible, connecting it with the chemical operations that caused the father's death; and also with '*Coppo* – eye-socket' (p. 230, note 1).

17 TN All references are to the Penguin edition of *Tales of Hoffmann*, trans. R.J. Hollingdale (1982). Where necessary I have also consulted *Der Sandmann* in the Deutscher Klassiker Verlag (1985).

18 TN Thus in English in the original.

19 Cf. *Moses and Monotheism*, SE, 23, p. 126.

20 Living music and dead language are opposed in the same way in *Der Dichter und der Komponist*: 'In the very moment of musical inspiration, every word and phrase would seem inadequate, dull and pitiful to him, and he [the composer] would be forced to descend from his heights, so as to be able to beg for the needs of his existence in the lowly region of words.' [TN. My translation from p. 81 of *Der Dichter und der Komponist* (in *Die Serapionsbrüder*, Selected Works (Winkler Verlag 1976).]

21 If one is concerned to preserve the opposition between form and subject matter that is at work in the Freudian text.

22 TN '*En abîme*'.

23 Cf. Freud, *A Seventeenth Century Demonological Neurosis*, SE 19, p. 86: 'When a boy draws a grotesque face and caricatures we may no doubt be able to show that he is jeering at his father in them.' We should also remember how important a role caricatures played in the life of Hoffmann himself.

24 Cf. The whole philosophical tradition for which the eye is the mirror of the soul: 'Art makes every one of its productions into a thousand-eyed Argus, whereby the inner soul and spirit is seen at every point' (Hegel, *Aesthetics* [trans. T.M. Knox (OUP 1975), chapter II, pp. 153–4]. Cf. also J.J. Rousseau's *Dictionnaire de Musique*, in which he defines imitation in music as the fact of having 'an eye in one's ear'.

25 Cf. Hoffmann's *Der Magnetisur*, in which the hero also has a dream that he is taken apart like a jointed doll and has his limbs tortured in all kinds of 'devilish experiments': 'Didn't another devilish anatomist [*anatomischer Satan*] once amuse himself by dismantling me like a doll and then carrying out all manner of devilish experiments? For example, seeing how it would look if I had a foot growing out of my neck or if my right arm was joined to my left foot?' [TN My translation from pp. 150 and 151 of *Der Magnetisur* in *Fantasie und Nachstücke*, Selected Works.]

A parallel can also be drawn with Bellmer's numerous disarticulated dolls.

26 TN My translation.

27 TN The French '*rouages*' stresses the link with '*roue*'.

28 This danger is proved by the fire that breaks out in the chemist's laboratory which, as if by chance, destroys the hero's lodgings. The son's destiny repeats the father's.

29 In *Der Dichter und der Komponist*, Hoffmann opposes the roaring torrent of music to the 'sterile sand' of words [ibid., p. 81]. A text I read after having written this essay.

30 For Descartes, one of the characteristics that distinguished the animal machine, the automaton, from the human being was its perfection. The subsequent comparison with clockwork is equally Cartesian.

31 Cf. pp. 109, 110, 114, 116.

32 The automaton that mimics the living creature is therefore no more apt than any other motif taken in isolation to produce *Unheimlichkeit*: a difference beween the perspective of the other students and Nathaniel's own, a satirical tone to the passage that Freud emphasizes: 'The episode of the automaton had struck deep roots into their souls and there stealthily arose in fact a detectable mistrust of the human form. To be convinced they were not in love with a wooden doll, many enamoured young men demanded that their young ladies should sing and dance in a less than perfect manner, that while being read to they should knit, sew . . . listen but sometimes speak too, and in such a way that what they said gave evidence of some real thinking and feeling behind it' (p. 121 of Hoffmann). Others of Hoffmann's stories give the theme of the automaton a comic treatment. For Bergson, a mechanism that mimics life, or a living being that mimics a machine, is even the comic theme *par excellence* (cf. *Le Rire*).

33 Just as the formal perfection of Nathaniel's poem, one that is particularly well constructed, pure and harmonious, conceals its diabolical inspiration.

34 The German term, '*starr*', is the same as that used to describe Olympia's appearance.

35 TN The French is '*pris dans une gangue de pierre lourde et froide*', a more accurate translation of the German '*al sei ich in schweren halten Stein eingepresst*' (p. 19), which conveys the sense of unnatural rigidity and paralysis.

36 The whole text would serve as a screen-memory designed to conceal the incestuous desire for the mother and its accompanying threat of death. The mother, who is the only integrated figure and one who must not be touched at any price, is, nevertheless, the image of death. For Freud's concealment of the link between incest and death, in which the castration complex plays the role of a screen-fantasy, cf. R. Barande, 'La

pulsion de mort comme non-transgression,' in *Revue Française de Psychanalyse* (June 1968).

37 'Because you sought to misuse your organ of sight for evil sensual pleasures, it is fitting that you should not see anything at all anymore' (Freud, *The Psychoanalytic View of Psychogenic Disturbance of Vision*, SE, 11, p. 217).

'The "punishment" of blinding turns out to be a retaliation [*Vergeltung*] for forbidden voyeuristic desires directed towards the mother and active castration or blinding fantasies about the father' (K. Abraham, *Psychoanalytische Studien*, ed. J. Cremerius, vol. I (S. Fischer Verlag 1971). [TN My translation from p. 334.]

38 'Thus voyeurism, through the limitation of sexual activity, can also take an increased significance. As a substitute for active sexual performance, there comes into being an intensified compulsion to look passively from a distance.' (ibid.). [TN My translation from p. 358.]

39 In turn Freud's insistence on the castration complex as the ultimate signified of the story plays down the importance of the theory of the death instinct: a theory that elsewhere he is in the process of promoting, since *Beyond the Pleasure Principle* dates from the same year.

40 *The Uncanny*, p. 232, note 1.

41 *A Seventeenth-Century Demonological Neurosis*, p. 86.

42 Cf. Kant, *The Critique of Judgement*, pp. 192 and 193. Kant defines eloquence as the art of deceiving by means of beautiful appearances. Hoffmann develops the idea of the diabolical power of eloquence further in *The Devil's Elixirs*.

43 In *Beyond the Pleasure Principle*, Freud states that all life tends to revert to inert matter. Death is life's *aim*, since the inert is its origin.

44 In *L'Enfance de L'Art* [translated as *The Childhood or Art*] we showed how a certain reading of Freud allowed the text to be seen as an originary double even before 1919, before the theory of the death instincts. However, only that theory gives such a notion its theoretical justification.

45 Cf. J. Derrida, 'Freud et la scène de l'ecriture', in *L'Ecriture et La Différance* (Seuil 1967) [translated as 'Freud and the scene of writing', in *Writing and Difference*, trans. Alan Bass (Routledge and Kegan Paul 1978)].

46 In this case, the devil would be a maternal rather than a

paternal figure. Rank drew attention to the fact that in the past the devil was feminine (quoted by A. Ehrenzweig in *The Hidden Order of Art*) [Weidenfeld & Nicolson 1967).

47 Freud, *Inhibitions, Symptoms and Anxiety*, SE, 20, p. 90.

48 Cf. *Medusa's Head*, SE, 18, p. 274.

49 Freud, *Inhibitions, Symptoms and Anxiety*, p. 89.

Index

Index by Meg Davies